STANLEY

KUBRICK

ON SCREEN

By Chris Wade

Stanley Kubrick On Screen by Chris Wade

Wisdom Twins Books, 2017

wisdomtwinsbooks.weebly.com

This edition released in 2017

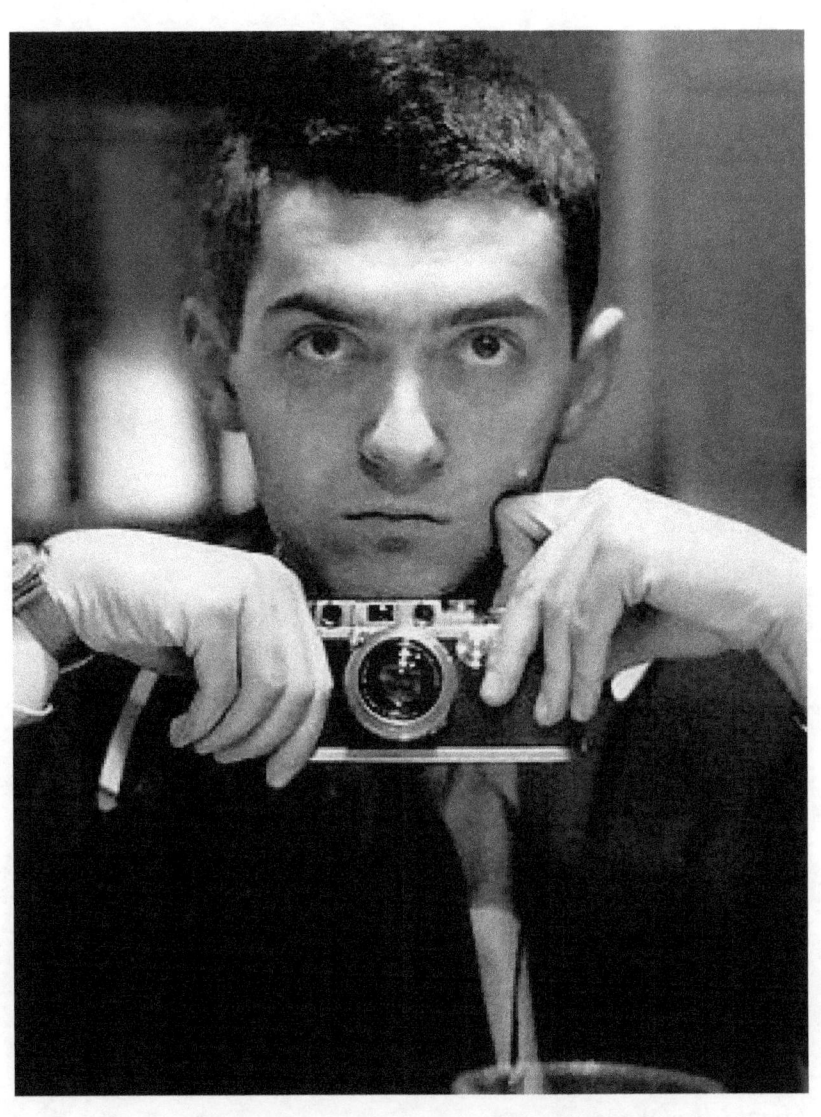

STANLEY KUBRICK
ON SCREEN

CONTENTS

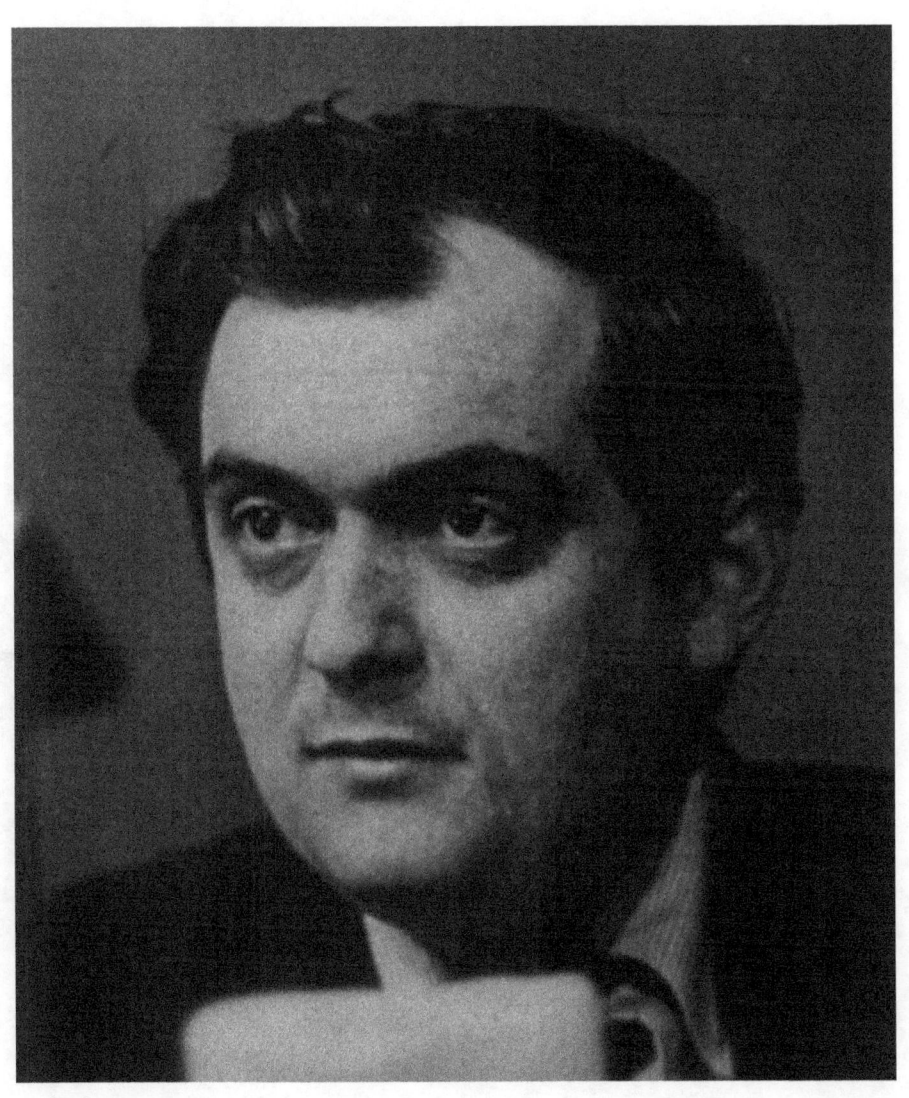

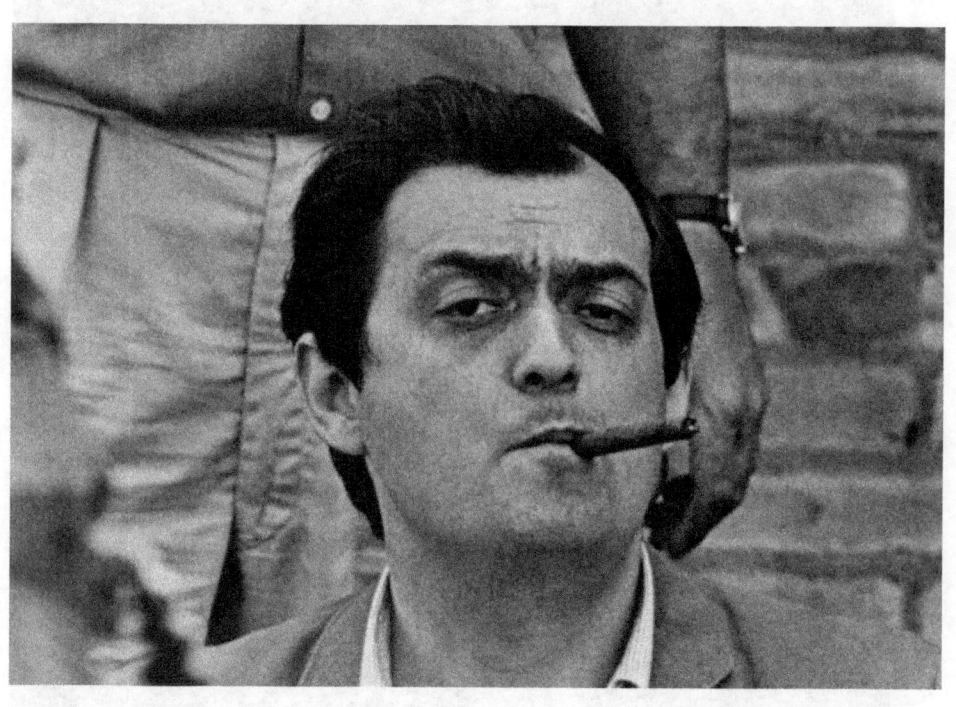

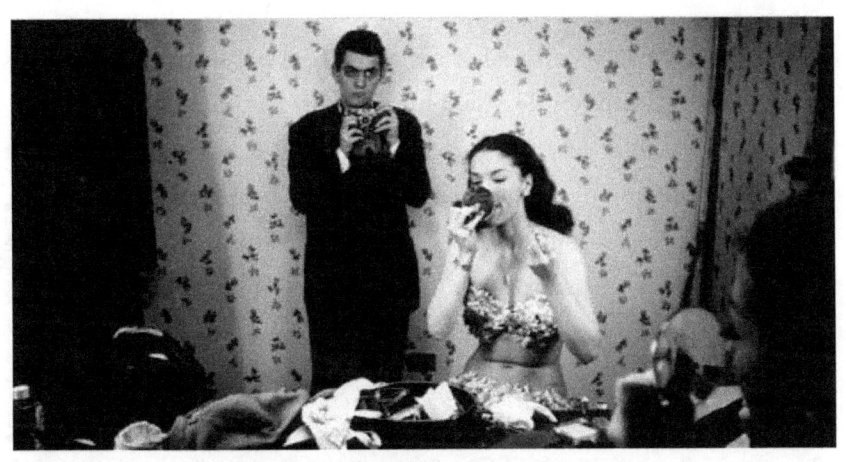

INTRODUCTION

"THE PHOTOGRAPH OF THE PHOTOGRAPH"

Stanley Kubrick is widely recognised as one of the greatest film makers in American history, a man who redefined every new genre he took on, influenced almost every director who came after him and changed the rule book forever. We say this about a lot of filmmakers these days, too many in fact, in an era where everyone and their grandma is apparently a legend. But Kubrick is from the old school of legend, the reclusive genius, the secretive perfectionist who lived in his own world, away from the spotlight, working from home, making movies and seeing to the running of his empire. A Napoleon for the film industry, he knew what he wanted and ruled over his productions with the firm authority of a general. He never did make that Napoleon biopic, but in a way he lived it.

That said, Kubrick was no evil dictator either. Close associates recall him as a funny man, and though merciless in his pursuit for perfection, Kubrick was kind, a caring father and loyal friend. "Fools didn't last long with Stanley" said his assistant Anthony Frewin.

Kubrick was one of those rare filmmakers, a complete maverick with total control over his own work, free from studio pressures, allowed to take as long as he felt like with his film projects. He worked his way up, starting out making short reel documentaries funded by family members before moving on to features. Fear and Desire was his debut, released in 1953, and though rough around the edges and later side lined by the man himself, it's an interesting glance into the young mind of a future innovator and visionary.

As the fifties went on, Kubrick sharpened his skills, eventually making his mark with The Killing (1956) and the startlingly gritty war epic Paths of Glory (1957), starring Kirk Douglas. It was the collaboration with this mega star which led Kubrick to his first major Hollywood work, 1960's Spartacus, for which Douglas hired him after firing the first director. Though he hated the experience, and loathed not being in control, it led him to eventually achieving true cinematic independence. Once established, he proved himself with a run of movies unmatched in their execution; Lolita, Dr. Strangelove, 2001: A Space Odyssey, A Clockwork Orange, Barry Lyndon, The Shining, Full Metal Jacket and Eyes Wide Shut. Though a small filmography when you measure it over the forty or so years it took them to surface, it's hard to make a single quibble about that list.

Stanley was born in New York, 1928. His father was a doctor, and he was keen on the young Kubrick following in his footsteps. As Stanley told one interviewer, "My parents had wanted me to be a doctor but I was such a misfit in high school that when I graduated I didn't have the marks to get into college." The medical profession wasn't for him.

As most Kubrick fans know, he first came to prominence as a young photographer for Look Magazine. It was the mid 1940s and he was still a teenager when he became an apprentice photographer for the magazine, while actively playing chess in parks for extra money to supplement his income.

"Like almost everything else good that's ever happened to me," Stanley later said, "by the sheerest stroke of good luck, I had a very good friend on Look magazine, a woman named Helen O'Brien, who was the picture editor. I knew her through selling two picture stories to Look that I had shot when I was still in high school. She asked me if I would like a job - you know, a junior photographer or something. They gave me a job, for $50 a week, as a still photographer. After about six months I was finally made a staff photographer. My highest salary was $105 a week. But I travelled around the country and I went to Europe. I learned a lot about people and things."

Though he has few true contemporaries, he can be matched up against one of his fellow mavericks. Born around the same time as Kubrick was the eccentric English filmmaker Ken Russell, who also made his name with startling photography in the 40s and 50s after his brief run as a ballet dancer. Ken captured the bohemian world of 50s England, while Kubrick captured America at a changing time, post-war, vibrant and booming with energy. When it came to filmmaking, both were masters of their craft, and though they shared a fondness for extravagance on film, they were drastically different beasts. In fact, no other director on earth can be compared to Stanley Kubrick.

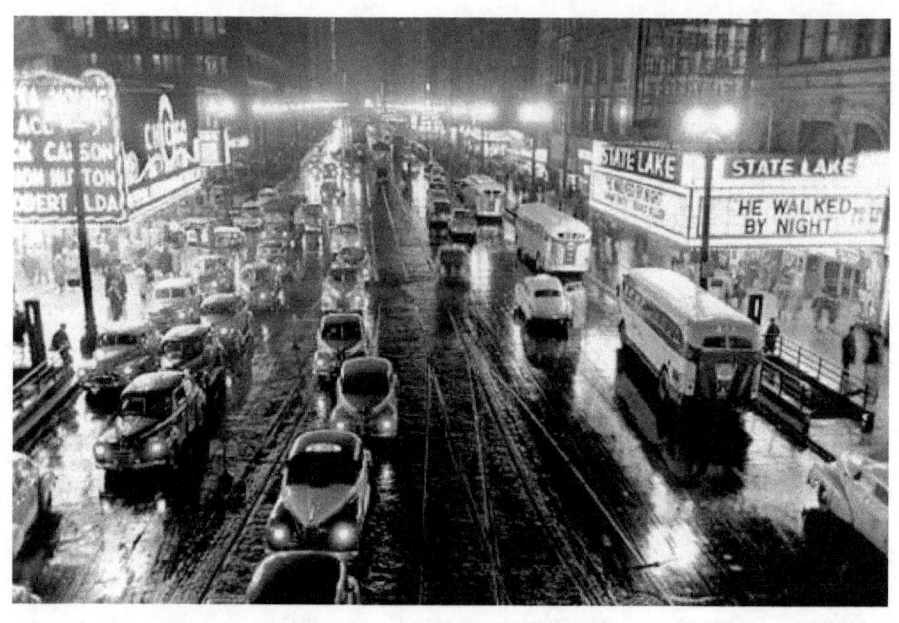

Stanley the photographer. Some of his shots for Look Magazine.

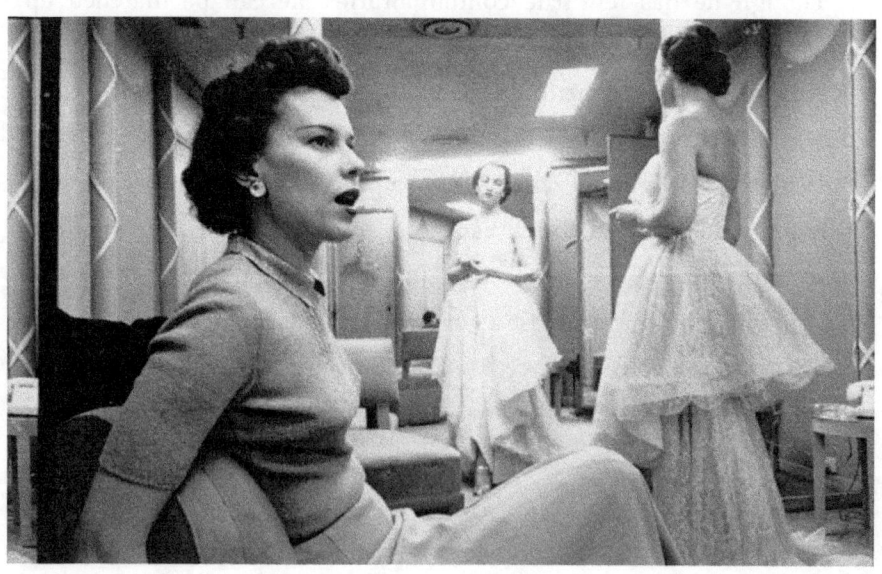

But all the masters started somewhere, and for Kubrick it was the still, not the moving image, that provided him with his first valuable work experience. The young Stanley was known for his photographs of famous jazz musicians, like Sinatra and Muggsy Spanier, startling images that come off bursting off the page before your eyes. It was inevitable by the dramatic set ups of each still, and the perfect composition, that Kubrick would one day be naturally drawn to the moving image as opposed to the merely static. It was in fact when covering a boxing match that he was inspired to move into cinema.

But photography is the key to grasping Kubrick's film work. His pictures were clearly from the eye of a seasoned photographer, each frame worthy of being hung on the wall of a gallery. Few, if any filmmakers have utilised the visual capabilities of film as Kubrick did, and even though he made very few films when considering the large time span his career covered, he left his mark with each and every one. What we remember most from his films are the images themselves, iconic as they are, and how they are presented to us. We recall Jack Nicholson, head popping through the splintered door yelling "Here's Johnny!" in The Shining; the slow motion Ape Man with his bone in 2001; the grizzly suicide in Full Metal Jacket; Cruise and Kidman, soon to be mistrusting husband and wife, naked before their bedroom mirror in Eyes Wide Shut; Malcolm McDowell as Alex DeLarge, supping calmly from a glass of Moloko Plus in the opening scene from A Clockwork Orange. I could ream off a full book's worth of memorable cinematic moments from Kubrick's canon, quite literally, and I would still only be scratching the surface. His perfectionism, notorious and mythical, may have driven his collaborators (or should that be underlings?) totally mad, but it was

11

worth it in the end; not just for the man's unmatched legacy, but for all our collective enjoyment. Had Kubrick not served his time as a photographer, it's possible he may not have become the most visually gifted filmmaker the world has ever seen. He might have become a professional chess player instead, and the world would have been a few classics films poorer.

This book goes through every Kubrick movie, defining what makes each one so special, timeless and innovative. From his short documentary film debut The Day of the Fight, to his final masterpiece Eyes Wide Shut, Kubrick showed himself to be that rare sort of filmmaker, where every shot, second and frame was vitally important and utterly unforgettable. It's a filmography as close to perfection as one can get; yet the fact that perfection itself is unobtainable was the biggest disappointment of all to Stanley Kubrick, and the most ironic of realisations for a so called perfectionist.

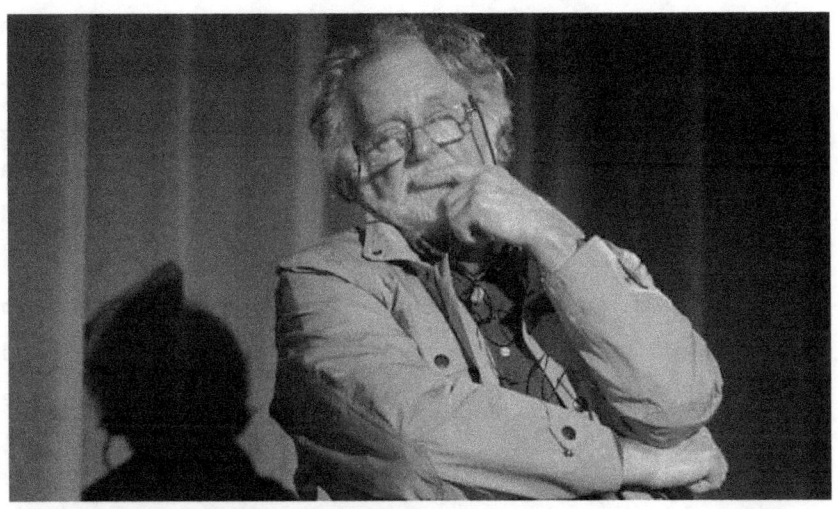

DOUG MILSOME

ON WORKING WITH STANLEY KUBRICK

Doug Milsome is a highly acclaimed cinematographer. He worked on a series of films with Stanley Kubrick, firstly as a camera operator on A Clockwork Orange, Barry Lyndon and The Shining, then as cinematographer on Full Metal Jacket. He spoke to me about the difficulties of working with Stanley on these landmark productions, and the technicalities involved in achieving the closest thing possible to perfection.

The first time you worked with Stanley was on A Clockwork Orange. How did you meet him, and do you recall your first meeting?

My first meeting with Stanley Kubrick was on set. I was chosen by John Alcott to replace a fellow camera member to complete the remaining few weeks of shooting. So little intro, hitting the ground running. I was daunted of course, being in the presence of greatness, his reputation preceding. Alcott briefed me. "Ego management, answer any question Yes, No or I'll Check. Don't make excuses. He's a chess player; play the pawn, he's like a dog with a bone!" I'd had previous experience before Clockwork Orange, remember. Fifteen years in camera working with Antonioni on Blow-Up, Joe Losey on Modesty Blaise, Polanski's Macbeth, Milos Foreman on Ragtime, and David Lean's Ryan's Daughter. Anyway, I was asked back for three more with Kubrick.

Barry Lyndon is one of the most visually beautiful films ever made. Was it difficult for everyone involved in the visuals to attain that level of excellence?

Like all of Kubrick's ideas, it's being a part of his creation. It was his idea to film in natural candlelight to achieve a luminance - if not impossible at the time - with artificial lighting with Kodak, using super high speed lenses. Difficult for me in particular. These lenses were produced by Zeiss for NASA's Apollo moon landing, and deep space photography designed for use on stills cameras. Kubrick got four or six, all 50mm... The task then became the long journey for the lenses to adapt to work with Stanley's 35mm BNC Mitchell non reflex motion picture camera. Many weeks later then to collimate and scale them to the correct point of focus - all my job.

Working at max aperture with such shallow depth of field proved exacting, and difficult in keeping candle light live action images in sharp focus. Anyway, the result evoked a genuine 18th Century atmosphere of pastel renaissance paintings and the best collection of images ever assembled on a single strip celluloid. a delicious feast for each eye.

The Shining is my favourite Kubrick film, probably my favourite movie ever made actually. How can you describe the vibe of the set? What was Kubrick like to work for on that film?

The vibe on set was easier, and less difficult technically for me than the 18 months spent on Barry Lyndon. I enjoyed being closer to Stanley, more understanding of his hard discipline, the pedantic perfection to his mind's eye and communicating with him at a level of trust. I grew more to admire him, and sometimes felt privileged to privately enjoy his off guard moments of humour. There was, alas, a price you paid being dedicated to Stanley Kubrick 24/7 - very little personal family life .

Did you have an idea you were all the part of making a special film with The Shining?

Like any other of his past movies, The Shining was no exception. A masterpiece of Modern Horror riding on the back of a best seller. Playful as it is hair raising, with Kubrick directing. It felt something special alright.

What are some of your favourite memories of working on The Shining?

Some of my favourite moments on The Shining were shared with Garrett Brown. inventor of the then little known Steadicam. Stanley Kubrick called it his magic carpet. Garrett's brilliant use of its execution was a cinematic breakthrough, capturing the blunt symmetry of endless corridors, patterned carpets, empty halls and doors. He could run with a 28lb camera with his rig flat   out, seamless to physical movement keeping the image rock steady.

A great guy. Happy memories. My other favourite moment was being chosen to complete the final principal photography for a further seven weeks after John Alcott left.. Also to shoot second unit photography in Oregon with Yan Harlan, his producer.

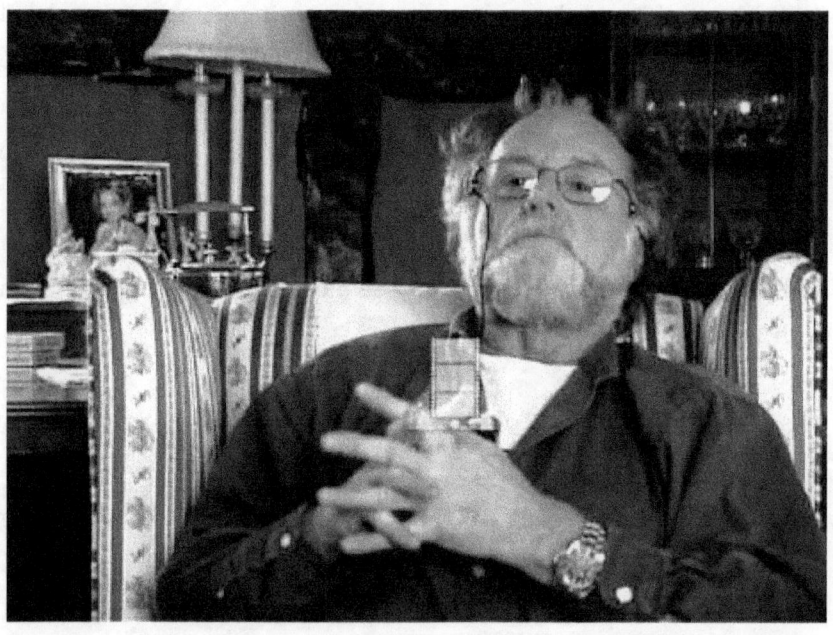

Full Metal Jacket is another film that looks stunning. Was it a challenging movie to film?

16

A tough shoot for all the crew, and for me as Cinematographer to please Kubrick into thinking he made the right choice in me.

What was you role in capturing the realism of combat on that film? Tom Savini, a war veteran told me it capture 'Nam better than any other film...

Vietnam's ruined city of Hue was shot in Dockland due for demolition. South East London was South East Asia; yet another idea of Stanley's, so we beat it up, adding palm trees for sub-tropical effect. We chose a look to shoot with low con fast film, heavily filtered, increased grain and colour. A study in grey/green back light smoke to evoke a mood of urban war. Stanley's plan was to mould his actors into a form he imagined; "born to kill" aggression on one hand, altruism on the other, creating confusion and a sense of hopelessness. And the actors not just knowing their scripted lines, but the interpretation and meaning behind the words. His iconic code - no heroes, no easy solutions, no happy endings.

What did you learn from working so closely with Kubrick on those seminal films that you could use in your career as a respected cinematographer?

What I learned? I suppose since Stanley died I have carried lots of memories of him. I continue to see a living memory of him in his films and their status as something special. As a cameraman, I tried to bring a reflection of his personal authorship, a perspective that becomes open to interpretation. Let the photography be true to the narrative, with camera movement not in the way of it.

How do you view his legacy?

Stanley's legacy, I feel, is style never replacing good ideas. Technique is no substitute for content, and the script. In my opinion, he made movies to get through a bad case of chronic anxiety disorder. He was never happier than being back behind the camera.

How does he compare to other directors you've worked with since? And do you see his influence a lot?

Actually I don't see his influence in other directors. There will never be another Stanley Kubrick! I'm 78 and I still miss him.

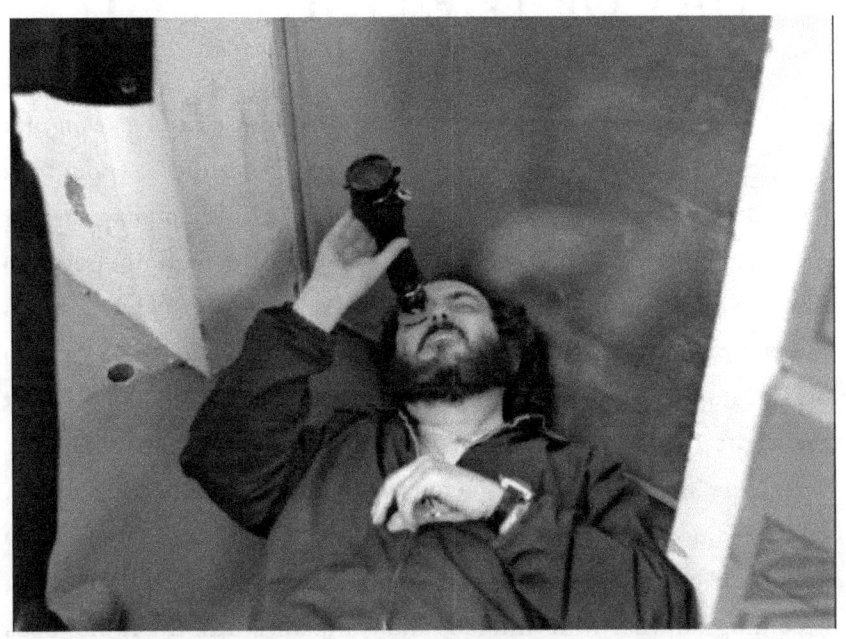

THE FILMS

"As Stanley would say, it's the films that matter, nothing else."
- Anthony Frewin, Kubrick's assistant,
to the author, 2017

DAY OF THE FIGHT (1951)

Right from the start, Stanley Kubrick showed himself to be a singular and unique force in bringing life to film, and film to life. Though he had already made his name in Look Magazine, photographing memorable images for decent pay, he had the itch to get into filmmaking, quitting his cosy salary for the lure of visual artistry. In the early 1950s, it was much harder to get a movie made, and to break into the film industry on any level. Sixty six years on, amidst the digital technological boom we live in, a film can be made for very little money on digital equipment. In 1951 though, Kubrick figured you would need five figure sums. He had some savings, 1500 dollars to be precise, and started getting out and about New York, becoming familiar with film labs and companies with the right goods. "I phoned places up," he said in 1966. "I checked the costs... It was something like, that I could do a documentary film, for 3500 dollars. Surely I must be able to sell them and get my money back."

Stanley Kubrick, out of school with few grades and harbouring the feeling that he didn't gain much at all from his short lived formal education, had entered working life through talent, luck and ambition. Though he regularly watched every movie that came across to New York at the theatres, he rarely got to see anything European or arty, as the art house era was a few years away in post-war America. Even so, he was inspired to get into film. Doing his homework and research, he was able to come up with a sum that was a tenth of what others were telling him it would cost to make a short movie.

"I was around twenty-one," Kubrick told Joseph Gelmis in a rare 1969 interview, telling the tale slightly differently. "I'd had my job with Look since I was seventeen, and I'd always been interested in films, but it never actually occurred to me to make a film on my own until I had a talk with a friend from high school, Alex Singer, who wanted to be a director himself (and has subsequently become one) and had plans for a film version of the Iliad. Alex was working as an office boy for The March of Time in those days, and he told me they spent forty thousand dollars making a one-reel documentary. A bit of simple calculation indicated that I could make a one reel documentary for about fifteen hundred. That's what gave me the financial confidence to make Day of the Fight. I was rather optimistic about expenses; the film cost me thirty-nine hundred. I sold it to RKO-Pathe for four thousand dollars, a hundred-dollar profit. They told me that was the most they'd ever paid for a short."

Day of the Fight itself is a startling debut, its stark black and white cinematography and brutal punch ups bringing to mind Martin Scorsese's 1980 masterpiece Raging Bull. Following the build up to a fight, we get up close and personal with boxer Walter Cartier. He wakes up in bed with his twin brother, roams the streets in a suit and bow tie, while the narrator, Douglas Edwards, goes through the ritualistic routine of a build up to a big match. Some of the images are unforgettable; the brothers in church for instance is a classic Kubrick moment, while the simplistic sequence of them making dinner, as the dog waits for scraps, is marvellous and simplistic.

As his manager prepares him for the fight, the tension mounts, the body tightens and the musical score is full of tension. Bobby James is his opponent, a fighter with a great record who Walter hasn't actually met yet, but soon will. Walter's brother makes the final preparations and before too long the gloves are on. Immediately, Walter is a changed man, "a fierce new person" as the narrator suggests, a beast let out of its cage. Then he's in the ring, squaring up to his opponent. Crowd reactions are surprisingly blood thirsty and fiendish, while the fight itself is slightly messy, but nicely filmed. The real spontaneity of the fists locking together is in great contrast to the earlier, calmer, slightly more staged scenes that built themselves to the big moment. In the end, Walter K.O's his opponent, and stands victorious. The film ends rather abruptly after the knock out.

In the days before the internet and deluxe DVDs, films like this were destined to be unseen, and could only be glimpsed upon via a few photographs in the odd book, or read about in a little mention here or there. Almost mythical in my mind as a young film buff, it's funny to think these rarities are no longer rare at all. In fact, some of the fun and mystique is gone in this digital age, but at the same time it's a blessing we get to see and enjoy these formerly lost gems.

Quality wise, Day of the Fight is very strong, with wonderful cinematography by Alexander Singer and, as you would expect, powerful direction from a young Stanley. Using Eyemo cameras to shoot the actual fight, Stanley and Alexander were reloading their 100 foot reels frantically to ensure they didn't miss a minute of the action. It was guerrilla filmmaking at its earliest and most raw, Kubrick shooting from below in the midst of the fight. Even at such an early stage, with a film career unimaginable at this point, Kubrick had at least fulfilled one dream - he had made a movie of his own, and a very good one at that. Given the budget was so tight and Kubrick had to utilise time and equipment to an almost hectic level, it's a miracle the film looks and feels so good. Undoubtedly, the presence of Douglas Edwards' voice, a familiar tone on American news at the time, adds a lot of realism and drama to proceedings, but even with the sound on mute, Day of the Fight is effective as a short drama in its own right, a seminal artefact for the ages.

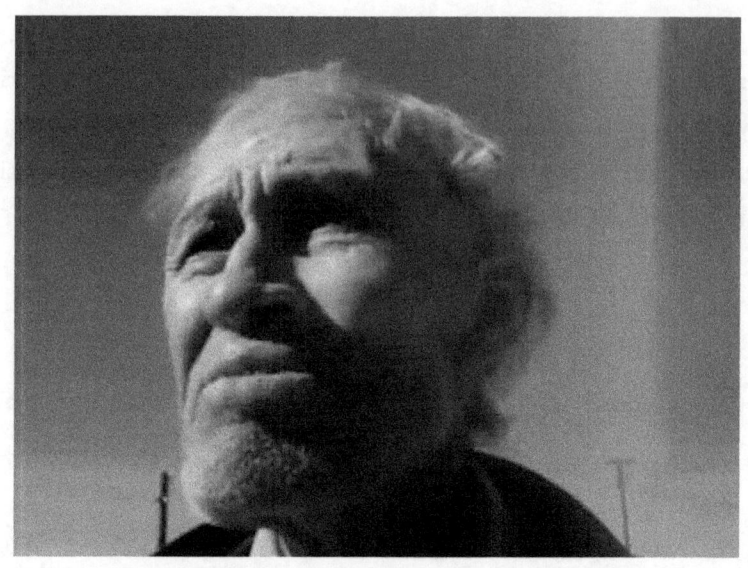

FLYING PADRE (1951)

Though shorter than his debut film, The Flying Padre was definitely still a sizeable advance in Kubrick's capabilities as a filmmaker and businessman. Having sold Day of the Fight to RKO and netting a 100 dollar profit for the deal, he found himself in no time at all being funded for a follow up film. RKO gave him an upfront fee to make his second short, and that turned out to be Flying Padre. Less memorable it may be, but it still boasts early signs of Kubrick's unmistakable visual flair. Though he couldn't orchestrate the real life incidents before his eyes, he could at least capture the beauty of a spontaneous moment, which is in some ways more of a challenge.

"I made one more short for RKO, The Flying Padre, on which I just barely broke even," Kubrick said in 1969, clearly dissatisfied with the film nearly twenty years on. "It was at this point that I formally quit my job at Look to work full time on filmmaking." He also referred to the film being "silly." Clearly, Kubrick's ambitions went far beyond 10 minute snapshots for RKO, and feature films were where his true passion lie.

The peculiar brief film follows Father Fred Stadtmuller, a Catholic priest in Mexico who gets about his vast 4000 square mile parish by the use of a small aeroplane, dubbed the Spirit of St. Joseph. Narrated

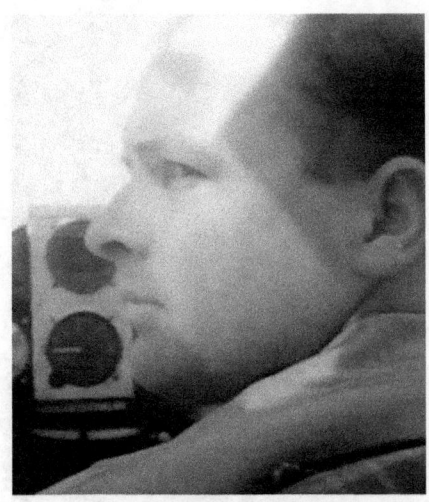

by famous CBS voice over artist Bob Hite, this typically early fifties tale is nicely shot, with Kubrick capturing the sparse landscapes, rustic homes, and pure, plain skies ethereally. The most dazzling sequence is when the priest covers a funeral, and Kubrick ensures we get bold, fearless close ups of the mourners, with every wrinkle in those lived in-faces shining right off the screen. Those people, now long dead themselves, will remain haunting forever, like the faces in a Fellini classic. Kubrick, though an acclaimed framer of scenes from wide shots, was also an expert in capturing the human soul as evident on the surface of the skin.

The padre himself is brilliantly captured too and comes across as an admirable hero of sorts, particularly when soaring in his aircraft. In my view he is one of the great unsung heroes in all of Kubrick's canon. So it's something of a joy to learn that he was still living out his duties until his death in 2008 at the grand old age of 95.

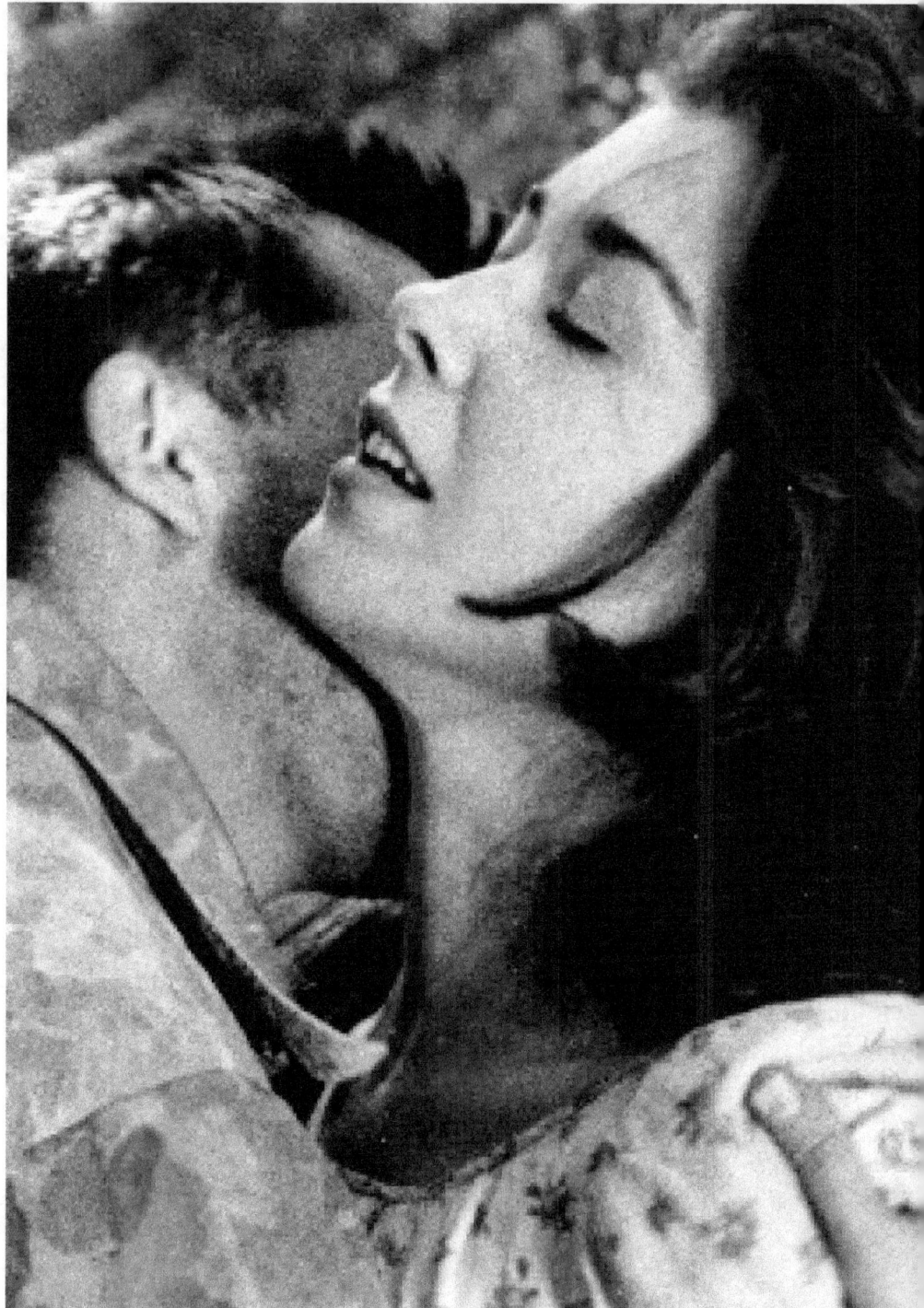

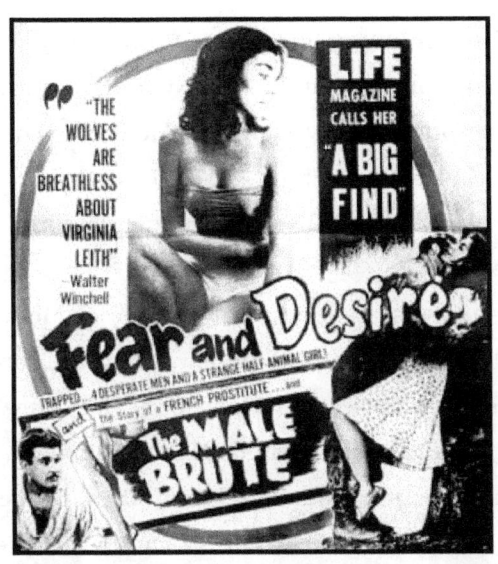

FEAR AND DESIRE (1953)

"There was no dolly track, just a baby carriage to move the camera. Stanley did all the shooting. No matter what the problem, Kubrick always seemed to have an answer. To me there was never a question that Stanley was already master of his universe."
- Paul Mazursky on the making of Fear and Desire

Like any young wide eyed film novice hoping to make his own masterpiece, Kubrick had to claw his way up the hard way. Even though he had made two shorts, Stanley was still at the very bottom, trying to gather funds for what would turn out to be Fear and Desire. Quitting his job at Look, he put all his energies into the movie.

Had Stanley been helped out largely by his parents, as is often the way with young talents trying to break into their desired area, he maybe could have indulged himself more freely, and thrown more money around the production. But cash was tight, much of it raised from friends and other family members. He had to cut corners from the word go, resulting in a tight schedule that didn't leave much room for freedom and indulgences, but taught him how to work under pressure. .

"Fear and Desire was made in the San Gabriel Mountains outside Los Angeles," he said in a 1969 interview. "I was the camera operator and director and just about everything else. Our "crew" consisted of three Mexican labourers who carried all the equipment. The film was shot in 35mm without a soundtrack and then dubbed by a post-synchronized technique. The dubbing was a big mistake on my part; the actual shooting cost of the film was nine thousand dollars but because I didn't know what I was doing with the soundtrack it cost me another thirty thousand. There were other things I did expensively and foolishly, because I just didn't have enough experience to know the proper and economical approach."

Stanley's criticisms of the film are harsh but valid. Though wonderfully shot, framed and composed, the dubbing is a major issue, though one can still enjoy the picture when putting aside the jarring sound. Written by Howard Sackler, it focuses on a war between two countries, neither of which are directly referred to in name. We follow four soldiers who have crashed behind enemy lines, and end up tying a local girl to a tree while figuring out a way to escape. Quite simply, as the title goes, the men wind up confronting their own fears and desires.

In its look and feel, Fear and Desire is haunting, atmospheric and rather eerie. Save for the often corny recitation of the script, and blatantly obvious overdubs, you wouldn't guess it was all shot for a mere (at the time) 33,000 dollars. Set ups are expertly staged as if by a seasoned pro, movement is clear and fluid, and Kubrick utilises the surrounding woodland and country side to great effect.

If Stanley had really initially aimed at a targeted budget of only 10,000, he was hopelessly optimistic. Borrowing most of the money from his uncle Martin, who owned and ran a pharmacy, he was good to his word and paid it all back. When the money got extra tight and Kubrick came into problems with some continuity and sound issues, he was given a hand by producer Richard de Rochemont, who helped sort out the issues under the promise Stanley would help out in his own subsequent TV special on Abraham Lincoln. Though not a seamless, smooth or fun experience, it was a massive learning curve for Kubrick. Only two years into his career as a filmmaker, he had made two shorts and a feature length movie, which is pretty remarkable given the constraints of filmmaking at that time.

Though Kubrick would later rubbish the film, it has its merits for sure. For one, the performance of Virginia Leith is exceptional, a startling portrayal of innocence considering how minimal the visible work really is. With the careless brutality of the soldiers, Leith appears even more wide eyed and hopeless, bringing to mind the poor Vietnamese victim in Brian De Palma's 1988 anti war statement, Casualties Of War. Kubrick said in print that he didn't think he got good performances from anyone in Fear and Desire, but I feel he was being unfair. On the poster, Virginia Leith is called "a big find," and she certainly was; it's a shame she never followed it up with solid work afterwards. Paul Mazursky, later an acclaimed director himself, handles the role of the weaker Private Sidney wonderfully, him being a classic Kubrick character with enough flaws and personal issues to fill a movie of his own.

The music seems a little over baked, but that's merely in retrospect. With the mood of films at the time, Gerald Fried's score was perfectly fitting for the over dramatic emphasis on key moments. The opening narration, provided by David Allen, is the only real flaw that affects it for me, and it should maybe have been dispensed with all together. With these minor niggles taken away, Fear and Desire is a solid, short piece of hidden treasure, and had Kubrick revisited the idea maybe ten or twenty years later, he could have made it another one of his masterpieces. In the book Stanley Kubrick: Director, Fear and Desire is only referred to very briefly, and in one segment is dubbed "a practice piece." The author considers it, alongside Spartacus - the latter which he dubs an assignment job - in an area outside the rest of Stanley's filmography. I agree that Fear and Desire is not as unified as later works, but it still has the Kubrick touch, look and feel, all in primitive forms of course.

Fear and Desire opened in 1953 on a small scale, seen as an art house picture and given the kind of distribution usually reserved for European or Avant-garde films. The film made very little money, but as Kubrick was to note, he garnered some nice reviews for his work.

"Fear and Desire, the drama fashioned by a tiny group of young, independent film makers, which arrived at the Guild Theatre yesterday," the New York Times wrote in April of 53. "For, in essaying a dissection of the minds of men under the stress of war, Stanley Kubrick, 24-year-old, producer-director-photographer, and his equally young and unheralded scenarist and cast, have succeeded in turning out a moody, often visually powerful study of subdued excitements.

If Fear and Desire is uneven and sometimes reveals an experimental rather than a polished exterior, its over-all effect is entirely worthy of the sincere effort put into it. Although its script is more intellectual than explosive and its cast more garrulous than mobile, Fear and Desire evolves as a thoughtful, often expressive and engrossing view of men who have 'travelled far from their private boundaries.' And it augurs well for the comparative tyros who made it."

Such words were no doubt encouraging to such a young director searching for his own voice in the movie world. Variety too were positive, and doffed their caps to the young and talented Stanley Kubrick: "Pic is work of Stanley Kubrick, who produced, directed, photographed and edited the film on a $100,000 shoestring budget. Film was written by 23-year-old poet Howard O. Sackler who has confected a blend of violence and philosophy, some of it half-baked, and some of it powerfully moving. Kubrick shot the entire film in the San Gabriel Mts and at a river at Bakersfield on the Coast, and he uses mists and tree leaves with telling effect. "

Still, even the slightly patronising, head patting reviews from major publications couldn't lift it above merely doing the small cinemas and making almost no business at all, not that one can judge artistic merit on commercial reception. On a personally financial level, it did Kubrick no favours, who had to go straight into doing a commission job, which his heart was hardly into. Adding to the unsatisfactory experience was the fact that, rather bizarrely, the film disappeared soon after its muted release. In a freak accident, the distributor of the movie, Joseph Burstyn, died in a plane crash the year the film was released, taking it speedily out of cinemas. It's been claimed in the past that Kubrick himself, the master of control and the same man who would self ban A Clockwork Orange from the country he later called his home (England), tracked down all known prints of Fear and Desire and kept them out of circulation. Even years later, when the film actually entered the public domain in the mid nineties, he was having none of it. He tried to bury it, downplay its importance and through Warner Brothers themselves, released the statement that Fear and Desire was a bumbling amateur film exercise. Only in the years following his death has it seen a resurgence in appreciation.

Even though the film is coming on to be 65 years old now, its themes are still relevant; like the emotionally stunted macho behaviour of the soldiers; the sense of shivering fear when in combat; the heartless sexism of the "brutes" towards the girl. The fact that the narrator pretty much tells us this could be "any war", one being fought in any time in any country, makes the film, in a fashion, timeless, despite its technical drawbacks which make its age all too obvious. But symbolically and thematically, this is a film that's message will always seem vital. All wars are equally vile, and there are multiple victims; not just the soldiers, but the innocent and helpless too.

Now in the public domain, and released in both DVD and Blu Ray editions, the film is clearly not just for the Kubrick fanatic to enjoy (as some critics and doubters of the film have claimed it to be); it's an interesting and note worthy film in its own right. Budding filmmakers could perhaps learn from it too, and take in the astonishing fact that if a young Stanley Kubrick could get together enough money to make a picture in an age before digital cameras and cheap editing programs, then so can you!

THE SEAFARERS (1953)

Of the three documentary films Kubrick made in his early years, 1953's The Seafarers is perhaps the most memorable and indicative of what Kubrick would go on to achieve in the coming decades. Significantly, on top of the fact that the film features Kubrickian scenarios and his iconic composition, this is his first dalliance with colour film; though he wouldn't use it again until 1960 with Spartacus, and then not permanently until 1968's 2001: A Space Odyssey onwards.

Kubrick made the movie for the Seafarers International Union in June of 1953, the very same year Fear and Desire emerged and sadly sank soon after. Like Fear and Desire, Seafarers was lost for quite some time and only resurfaced (nautical puns unintended) in the 1970s when discovered by a chap named Frank P Tomasulo. The Seafarers, for me at least, is the most valuable piece in the whole of Kubrick's earliest years. The shots are imaginative, there is a cinematic quality to the way he captures the Seafarers in their everyday lives and even a dolly shot, itself a classic technique in the Kubrick box of tricks. Even if Kubrick himself had little regard for it, there is a lot to treasure for the Kubrick student here. Yet one cannot blame Stanley for brushing the film's personal unimportance aside. After all, this was a commissioned piece, made for money alone in order to merely pay bills and fund the next feature length picture, after the underwhelming reaction to Fear and Desire.

Despite this, Stanley must have enjoyed shooting something totally different for a change, this time out at sea. He certainly captures the social scene in the cafe well, highlighting the camaraderie and sense of family out there in the ocean. There are some truly wonderful shots of interaction between the men, and Kubrick ensures each angle is engaging, each cut artful despite the "unarty" subject matter. Note also the often breathtaking shots of ships, the vast sea and how he manages to show us, with simplistic ease, the sheer scale of the seafaring life. Again, the inevitable need for straight faced narration, this time by the very serious Don Hollenbeck, ages the film somewhat, but also makes it a typical document of its time.

Kubrick never mentioned The Seafarers in any of his interviews, and it seems to have been totally forgotten by most film fans. Day of the Fight is certainly his most celebrated early short, but I find The Seafarers more inspired, widened and neatly executed in bringing together the different aspects of this somewhat alien world. As a commissioned piece, it's a success; and as a document showing us early signs of future genius, it's invaluable and fascinating.

KILLER'S KISS (1955)

Commissions and documentaries were still of very little interest to Stanley Kubrick in the mid 1950s, but he knew they were essential in keeping his dreams of being a filmmaker afloat. In modern times, Kubrick would have simply nipped out and bought himself a nice digital camcorder and a cheap editing suite, and got to work on a low budget film of his own which he could control from start to finish. But the mid 1950s were a very different time for the budding director, and funds had to be raised the hard way; through begging and pleading to friends and family. But this wouldn't be so easy, especially when you consider the financial failure of Fear and Desire.

Again the script was by Howard Sackler, who had contributed the screenplay for Fear and Desire. Revisiting the boxing theme of Day of the Fight, the 67 minute thriller covers all kinds of areas in its brief, swiftly paced running time. The film follows boxer Davey Gordon (played by Jamie Smith), who is coming close to the end of his career. Davey gets involved with taxi dancer Gloria (Irene Kane) who is fighting off advances from her boss, Vincent (played by Frank Silvera), and confronts the man, who quickly flees. As Davey and Gloria begin a relationship, Vincent proves to be an ever looming presence. Eventually, he and his goons kidnap Gloria, holding her hostage, and inevitably the problems and complications mount as the film builds to its climax.

In 1962, Terry Southern interviewed Kubrick about his then latest picture Lolita, but Stanley also went into his earliest films. "Yes, a pretentious, inept and boring film - a youthful mistake costing about

50,000 dollars," he said, firstly of Fear and Desire, but going on to explain the genesis of Killer's Kiss. "But it was distributed by Joseph Burstyn, in the art houses and caused a little ripple of publicity and attention. I mean there were people around who found some good things in it, and on the strength of that I was able to raise private financing to make a second feature-length film, Killer's Kiss. And that was a silly story too, but my concern was still in getting experience and simply functioning in the medium, so the content of a story seemed secondary to me. I just took the line of least resistance, whatever story came to hand. And for another thing I had no money to live on at the time, much less to buy good story material with - nor did I have the time to work it into shape - and I didn't want to take a job, and get off the track, so I had to keep moving. Fortunately too, I wasn't offered any jobs during this period - I mean perhaps if I had been offered some half-assed TV job of something I wouldn't have had the sense to turn it down and would have been thrown off the track of what I really wanted to do, but it didn't happen that way. In any case, I made that picture Killer's Kiss, and United Artists saw it and bought it."

Story was to become the big obsession for Kubrick in his established years, and he could spend years searching for the right one. In his early days however, he had to take what story was offered his way. Despite this, Killer's Kiss was the first truly important film Kubrick had put his name to, even if it wasn't at all the kind of thing he really wanted to do, and one he would later overlook. The budget was much larger at 75,000 and there was more responsibility riding on it achieving a level of success. In some ways, it was make or break for Stanley, who needed a hit and to get his foot in the door of the business. When he sold Killer's Kiss to United Artists for 100,000, he made a significant leap, though he had to make some strict compromises in order to be welcomed into the Hollywood machine. For one, the studio required a happy ending. Though it killed Kubrick to bow to the studio's pressure, he didn't yet have the clout to stand his ground and assure them that *he* knew best. With only one unsuccessful picture behind him, to them he knew very little. Even though Kubrick's integrity took a few blows in this early stage, these unsatisfactory experiences were invaluable lessons in how he would conduct his future affairs, once he had the power to rule his art.

Despite Kubrick dismissing the picture in later years, Killer's Kiss (originally called The Nymph and the Maniac, more like a Ken Russell title) actually has a lot going for it, and offers what was a new and unique slant on the 1950s crime flick. Again, there's a delicate beauty to the framing and the composition, with Kubrick using shots and ideas that weren't so heavily featured in cinema of that age. The soundtrack, though featuring dubbing again, is much smoother, and the choice of music, a nice score by Gerald Fried, makes all the right moves, establishing correct moods throughout. Though the sound was actually recorded at the time of filming, Stanley was dissatisfied with the results and redubbed the whole movie afterwards, a process which took him months of frustrating work. It proved that even then he was committed to getting things just right.

My own personal favourite scenes in the film are the stark and brutal boxing sequences, which once again, like Day of the Fight, bare more than a little resemblance to those in Martin Scorsese's Raging Bull. Seeing as Raging Bull covered boxing legend Jake La Motta's fighting experiences in the very era Killer's Kiss was made, it's no surprise that Scorsese himself sought inspiration from these excellently executed scenes. They are compelling fights, no doubt about it, and Kubrick takes you right inside the ring so you feel every single punch. Even without the freedom and extravagance of a larger budget and more time on his hands, he could still pull off staggering moments like this.

The hard work paid off, this time much more fruitfully as it had on past projects. When UA bought the picture, they also promised to put up another 100,000 for Stanley's next film. The reception was much better than the one garnered by Fear and Desire, but Kubrick still had a long way to go. In truth, this film did have a few moments of shining glory, and is useful now as a historical piece and a document on how one of the world's finest filmmakers worked his way up, but at the time it was just another low budget crime film with noir-ish elements. Nicely filmed and all, it would have been ideal fodder for drive in theatres, where viewers would have cared very little for the lighting techniques, the cinematography or the imaginative shots., let alone the director's name. The plot would have been the real focus, and it was a plot that wasn't exactly close to Kubrick's heart. The man we all know as one of the ultimate personal filmmakers, who would spend anywhere from two, five or more years preparing a new project, was a long way away.

Reviews at the time were slightly underwhelming. Variety wrote: "Ex-Look photographer Stanley Kubrick turned out Killer's Kiss on the proverbial shoestring. Kiss was more than a warm-up for Kubrick's talents, for not only did he co-produce but he directed, photographed and edited the venture from his own screenplay (originally written by Howard O. Sackler) and original story. Familiar plot of boy-meets-girl finds small time fighter Jamie Smith striking up a romance with taxi dancer Irene Kane. Kubrick's low-key lensing occasionally catches the flavour of the seamy side of Gotham life. His scenes of tawdry Broadway, gloomy tenements and grotesque brick-and-stone structures that make up Manhattan's downtown eastside loft district help offset the script's deficiencies."

Retrospectively, when it *is* ever singled out, it's cited as a distinct point at which Kubrick started to really grasp at his own style, standing out from the mid fifties crowd. The dialogue and human interaction was handled well, but Kubrick shone the brightest as a director in Killer's Kiss when establishing mood, casting shadows, building tension and depicting action and movement. Again, like with many of Kubrick's later films, Barry Lyndon being a prime example, we value the images themselves rather than plot development. With sound being a difficult area for Stanley's early works, we find a man more preoccupied with giving the best visuals he can, and the sharpest you could hope for as a viewer. Killer's Kiss is a way off genius, but it contains enough gold to excite the film lover in us all, and offer a taste of what was to come in the world of Kubrick in the following decades.

THE KILLING (1956)

"Such a perfectionist was Kubrick that he knew every theatre his films were opening in, and the daily grosses. It's said that a projectionist in Kansas City received a phone call from Kubrick in England, informing him that the picture was out of focus. Is that story apocryphal? I've never thought so." - Roger Ebert, 2012

Though the films that came before this still have their merits, The Killing is well and truly the start of Stanley Kubrick's career as a solid filmmaker with his own voice and a reputation that began building with each subsequent picture. With name actors like Sterling Hayden attached, it was clear that Kubrick had moved up a gear from the ultra low budgets (for the time) of Fear and Desire and Killer's Kiss.

The big turn around came by a chance meeting with a producer by the name of James B. Harris. The pair had met in Washington Square where the young Stanley was supplementing his income by playing chess. Immediately struck by his intelligence, Harris and Kubrick hit it off. In no time at all, it became clear that Harris wanted to work with the sharp director on a new venture. He had recently sold his own distribution company, and was keen on developing a new hot talent. Kubrick was the man who fit the bill.

"He was running a television distribution company at the time," Kubrick said of Harris. "Together we made The Killing. That's the first film I made with decent actors, a professional crew, and under the proper circumstances. It was the first really good film I made, and it got a certain amount of attention."

With the rights to Lionel White's novel Clean Break bought, it was thought that a star name would make the film an actual possibility rather than a minor consideration for a studio. Sterling Hayden was signed up, but not considered starry enough for United Artists, so the rest of the money had to be put up by Harris himself - the total of 80,000 dollars - from his own pocket and a further 20 or so from his father. It was a big gamble for Harris, who was riding a lot on the picture being a success; but he clearly believed in Stanley.

Speaking to Film Comment, Harris reflected on his early meetings with Kubrick: "In the Army I met Alexander Singer when we were being trained as combat photographers, and Alex Singer had been a boyhood friend, and was still a friend, of Stanley Kubrick. He introduced me to Stanley at some point, and after I got out of the Army, I ran into him again, and he invited me to a screening of his latest film at that time, which was Killer's Kiss - he had previously done Fear and Desire. I was quite impressed with what he had done. I was back in the distribution business, producing television. Kubrick was interested in putting his films on TV and thought that maybe I could be the distributor. It was revealed that his film couldn't be cleared because it was tied up in litigation with the distributor that handled Fear and Desire. The producer, Joe Burstyn, had died in a plane crash, and therefore the film was tied up, and Stanley couldn't deliver it for me to distribute it on TV. We decided that there was really nothing we could do in that regard, so we talked about maybe getting together, I'd become a producer and he'd become a director with me. That's what we decided on, and formed Harris-Kubrick Pictures, and the rest, as they say, is history."

Harris said he bought the book from a place called Scribner's, struck by the plot (about a robbery on a race track) and its cinematic possibilities. For the screenplay, dialogue was handed over to novelist Jim Thompson, which proved to be a smart move. Original dialogue was not Stanley's strong point (Stanley would be the first to admit this) and he worked so much better when co-writing, collaborating or even lifting straight from the novel he happened to be adapting. So with the script firmly in place by a seasoned writer of crime fiction, Kubrick was free to bring the film to life on a visual level alone. It was in essence the start of his career as a serious filmmaker.

The Killing was actually well ahead of its time in regards to its structure. Taking on a more novelistic approach, the film plays with time and the placing of key events, plus character perspectives, as the likes of Tarantino and his elk would to great acclaim in the 1990s. Not just another entry in the heist genre, The Killing shakes up the already tired conventions; its jagged cutting is innovative, but was challenging for fifties audiences. Stylishly shot, it's aged very well. Rightfully so, it acted as a great calling card for Stanley Kubrick the filmmaker, no longer Stanley Kubrick the chess player, photographer and some time filmmaker. He had, in a small way, arrived.

Unfortunately, the film didn't do good business, failing to get a full US release and only put out as a second feature in a double bill with Bandido. There were good reviews though, and Kubrick was now a name on the lips of many people.

"Though The Killing is composed of familiar ingredients and it calls for fuller explanations, it evolves as a fairly diverting melodrama," New York Times wrote at the time. "Stanley Kubrick, the film's youthful director, who also wrote the script, was not being niggardly in his stakes. Mr. Kubrick has kept things moving at a lively clip as the plotting is revealed in timetable fashion. Sterling Hayden makes a restrained but hard and efficient leader. His Johnny Clay is a tough citizen who knows the dangers his boys will face and he takes no chances. Elisha Cook does well by the role of a Caspar Milquetoast of a race-track cashier who is willing to risk his neck to buy the love of his wife. As that two-timer, Marie Windsor is properly cheap, brassy and decorative. Aficionados of the sport of kings will discover that Mr. Kubrick's cameras have captured some colourful shots of the ponies at Bay Meadows track. Other observers should find The Killing an engrossing little adventure. Chances are it will be less exhausting than a day at the track."

The film wasn't smoothly received by everyone. "There were walkouts at the preview," Harris told Director's Guild. "People didn't know what they were going to see, and were confused. Sterling Hayden's agent told us we'd wrecked the picture. Even friends advised us to make it more conventional. Stanley and I asked ourselves, 'Have we blown it?' We rented an editing room and built a linear cut of the picture. Halfway through screening it for ourselves, we looked at each other and said, 'This stinks. Let's put it back the way we had it.' You've got to believe in your own instincts. If you listen to hostile voices, even those of friends, you shouldn't make movies. If you're going to fail, fail with your own contributions, not somebody else's. Lesson learned!"

Sterling Hayden himself puts in a great performance, a visually strong actor who commands the screen from the word go. Asked years later about what Kubrick saw in him for the part, a heavily bearded Hayden replied, "Oh man... maybe what I know of life now.

Why is a man a hoodlum? A two bit hood. Maybe the weakness, which is part of it; it takes a certain weakness to be a crook as well as courage. I don't know. Everything's confused. Maybe he felt... I dunno, maybe he felt he could get something. I don't know." Though not enlightening in a literal way, Hayden's reply does capture the enigmatic mystique of Kubrick. No one truly knew what he was thinking or where he got his inspiration from, even his first star.

Though there are shades of classic Kubrick here, and even as you admit it really was the first fully formed Kubrick movie, it still could have been done by any number of decent directors at the time with European sensibilities, taking extra care for each shot and its visual impact. The difference was in the structure and the more artsy approach to what could have been a standard pot boiler. Directly influencing Tarantino's Reservoir Dogs, the 1990s wunderkind even said in one interview, "I didn't go out of my way to do a rip-off of The Killing, but I did think of it as my Killing, my take on that kind of heist."

"It's tempting to search here for themes and a style he would return to in his later masterpieces," Roger Ebert rightly noted in his 2012 piece on the film, "but few directors seemed so determined to make every one of his films an individual, free-standing work. Seeing it without his credit, would you guess it was by Kubrick? Would you connect Dr. Strangelove with Barry Lyndon?" Probably not is the answer, but that's more down to Kubrick's cinematic shape shifting than anything else. But Ebert managed to nail the appeal of Kubrick in one sentence, perhaps unknowingly as it goes. The fact that each film was so drastically different from the last stopped people getting bored of his work, and made categorising him utterly impossible.

Each movie was an event, coming every few years to unprecedented hype and excitement. The Killing, in the hands of any other director, could have been a straight forward heist thriller, a B movie that happened to have a minor star in it. But Kubrick, and Harris too, dared to be different, challenging the formula and trying things from a different angle.

As it turned out so far, he had only scratched the surface of what cinema could achieve; but in time, he would explore its every conceivable possibility.

PATHS OF GLORY (1957)

Kubrick returned to the book shelf for inspiration for his next film, Paths of Glory, one of the boldest war films from its era. Visually striking, rich and painfully raw for its time, it's inspired countless films depicting battle since its release sixty years ago. Without it, the gut wrenching opening battle of Spielberg's Saving Private Ryan would not exist, and the swirling chaos of Francis Ford Coppola's Apocalypse Now would be a shadow of what it is. Shot in stark black and white, it is by far Kubrick's most powerful film up to that point, rivalling his iconic work from the sixties onwards. It remains one of his finest films.

As anti war statements go, Paths of Glory could possibly be paired up with another film Kubrick made exactly thirty years later, the Vietnam flick Full Metal Jacket. In fact, these are perhaps the only two films in his canon which have anything in common at all, though they are still drastically different. Full Metal Jacket was later sixties 'Nam; Paths of Glory focuses on World War 1, with Kirk Douglas taking on the lead role of Colonel Dax, who rules over a troop of French soldiers who dare to question authority and see the suicidal pointlessness of going over the top, out of the trenches and into certain death. Kubrick is raging in his statement that the generals have no regard for the infantry, and though it's obvious from reel one what his intention is, the message is inevitably more honest and bare boned when not hidden behind arty metaphors.

Written by Humphrey Cobb as a novel, it was first published in 1935. A WW1 veteran himself, Cobb fought for the Canadian army and went on to d a series of jobs, one of them writing this landmark novel. He died in 1944, with Paths of Glory being his only famous work. It had first been attempted as play, but Kubrick read the book and bought the film rights from Cobb's widow for a reported $10,000. Based loosely on true events, where a group of French soldiers were court marshalled for refusing orders, the book was a powerful, daring work that stood up against the injustice of the military regime and its heartless ethics. This aspect of the book undoubtedly interested Kubrick, a man so concerned, in his later films more so, with the plight of the "little man" in the face of the machine. Whether that machine was the military, the government, or any other powerful organisation didn't seem to matter; we are all ruled in some way.

Stanley later explained his brave decision to do a war film, clearly fascinated by the inevitable conflict which man chooses to become entangled in. "One of the attractions of a war or crime story is that it provides an almost unique opportunity to contrast an individual or our contemporary society with a solid framework of accepted value, which the audience becomes fully aware of, and which can be used as a counterpoint to a human, individual, emotional situation," he said. "Further, war acts as a kind of hothouse for forced, quick breeding of attitudes and feelings. Attitudes crystallise and come out into the open. Conflict is natural, when it would in a less critical situation have to be introduced almost as a contrivance, and would thus appeared forced or, even worse, false."

Like his Alex De Large in A Clockwork Orange, Douglas's Dax is but one individual, standing against the vast, throbbing power of the establishment. Even with as much authority and influence he believes he has, he is utterly powerless when push comes to shove.

In the book Stanley Kubrick: Director, Kubrick friend and film critic Alexander Walker called Paths of Glory, "Kubrick's graduation piece," the moment he stepped up from being an "interesting newcomer" making low budget thrillers and into being a "significant" director in his own right. Paths of Glory is a classy picture, shot with grace and a sense of confidence in the heavy load. There are some truly stunning sequences which, with their sense of realness and unflinching brutality, set them apart from all the other war films from that time - and there were a few. Paths of Glory puts you right there, more so than any of the classic pictures covering that war. In fact, it can only be compared to Lewis Milestone's 1930 classic All Quiet on the Western Front, released nearly thirty years earlier, for its sense of earth shattering power.

Originally, no one in Hollywood was particularly interested in making the picture until Kirk Douglas signed up for the lead. Before then, Kubrick was at MGM "developing" scripts and ideas for the studio, but the company saw no potential in Paths of Glory and thought it would flop. In the end, it was United Artists who signed Stanley up, and the film was under way.

Filming was done in Bavaria, Germany, budgeted at 1 million dollars, which doesn't sound much today but was actually a sizeable amount back then; especially to Kubrick, whose first features hadn't even cost $100,000. The soldiers were given an authentic look, and Kubrick went to great lengths in making sure everything reeked of the war. It was the beginning of Kubrick's obsession to detail, only the parameters were not yet wide enough for him to perform the kind of research and preparation he truly desired.

"We employed approximately eight hundred men, all German police," Kubrick said, "at that time the German police received three years of military training, and were as good as regular soldiers for our purposes. We shot the film at Geiselgesteig Studios in Munich, and both the battle site and the chateau were within thirty-five to forty minutes of the studio."

At the centre of this bold and daring film is one of Kirk Douglas's meatiest and most precise performances. Already a star in his own right, he had wowed the world with his terrific portrayal of Vincent Van Gogh in Lust for Life, and in the same year he made Paths of Glory would also have hits with The Vikings and Gunfight at the OK Coral. A very commanding figure, both physically and in his acting approach, it's hard to imagine anyone else in the role. As with most of Kubrick's truly great films, it's impossible to substitute the face of the lead actor in your mind for another. Think of Malcolm McDowell's iconic side grin in A Clockwork Orange and you realise that the film wouldn't have worked with anyone else in the part, and Kubrick knew this. Now picture The Shining without Jack Nicholson, Eyes Wide Shut without Cruise and Kidman, or Dr Strangelove without Peter Sellers. Kubrick definitely knew how to cast a feature.

"A director can't get anything out of an actor that he doesn't already have," Kubrick explained when the point of Douglas's performance came up in one interview. "You can't start an acting school in the middle of making a film. Kirk is a good actor."

The movie was well received upon release, garnering BAFTA nominations and acclaim, but it wasn't without its controversy either. French war veterans called for the film to be banned in their home country, and indeed it was pulled until the mid seventies. As an anti war film, and not merely a piece of gung ho entertainment, it was decades ahead of its time. Even during the Vietnam War around ten years later, there were no real loud cinematic opposing statements to the conflict, and most of the truly great anti-'Nam flicks came in the 1970s and 80s. By then, independent cinema and the New Hollywood boom of 69 meant that the barriers of filmmaking had widened, and the envelope could be pushed more. Films could say something about the establishment and get away with it by then, and in fact were often applauded for doing so. The sixties liberated creative people all over the world to get their messages out in the form of entertainment. In 1957 though, Hollywood ruled, and they wanted hits with happy endings. Paths of Glory, then, was way ahead of the game, and it was Kubrick who dared to push it that bit further.

Not all the reviews of the time were glowing though. "Mr. Kubrick has made it look terrific," the New York Times wrote in a mixed review. "The execution scene is one of the most craftily directed and emotionally lacerating that we have ever seen. But there are two troubling flaws in this picture, one in the realm of technique and the other in the realm of significance, which determine its larger, lasting worth. We feel that Mr. Kubrick—and Mr. Douglas—have made a damaging mistake in playing it in colloquial English, with American accents and attitudes, while studiously making it look as much as possible like a document of the French Army in World War I. The illusion of reality is blown completely whenever anybody talks. As for the picture's significance, it comes to an inconclusive point. Its demonstration of injustice is like an exhibit in a bottle in a medical museum. It is grotesque, appalling, nauseating - but so framed and isolated that, when you come away, you are left with the feeling that you have been witness to nothing more than a horribly freakish incident. Also, merely as a footnote - what a picture to open on Christmas Day!"

However, when it was re-released on the 100th anniversary of the outbreak of World War 1, it was reappraised as a classic. The Guardian raved about the film, writing, "It is arguably the best film about the first world war, and still has a reasonable claim to being Stanley Kubrick's best film." A bold statement indeed.

Paths of Glory is the first Kubrick film where images and scenes immediately pop into your head when you think of the film. The sequence which I always come back to is when Dax storms through the trench, the sound of gunfire echoes around, and the men stand like contorted statues; slumped over, resembling lifeless, melting wax works, their eyes dead and souls empty. They cower from the smoke and dust, but Dax is unflinching in the face of the terror, keeping his cool, and his head high. Then they go over the top, whistles blowing, in one of the most blistering, searing and shiver inducing battle sequences ever filmed. In true Kubrick style, we track the soldiers as they advance, the camera gliding through the barren wasteland, broken wood and barb wire. The men are dropping like flies, but Douglas leads on, defiantly, as bombs explode around him and men plunge at his feet, through water, mud and debris. It's a remarkable, stunning scene, and without it the war genre would not be the same. The nightmare battles of Apocalypse Now and Saving Private Ryan, to merely name two pictures, wouldn't exist without it.

It's not just the combat sequences which stick in the mind though. The scenes with the generals are some of the most powerful too, especially when Dax squares up to the vile and sadistic Major

Broulard. Kirk shows his real acting chops in these sequences, embodying a nation's collective anger against the stony faced arrogance of the commanding officers. For me though, and thousands of other viewers, the most moving and effective sequence comes near the end, when the soldiers, rowdy and drunk, are revelling at a bar. Christiane Harlan, soon to become Christiane Kubrick, plays an imprisoned German girl, who captures the men's imaginations by singing an old folk song. At first, they holler and guffaw as she sings her gentle melody, but their raucous laughter dies down until eventually they are in utter silence, listening to the sweet voice of the innocent girl. She represents purity and honesty in a time where those things don't seem to even exist. Cleansed by her song, they remain transfixed, moved, still to the spot. Dax, knowing that the men have to go back to the front, says nothing and lets them enjoy their brief moment of undisturbed peace. It's one of the most touching, sad and poignant moments from any war film, and it makes its point without dialogue, only mild mannerisms, simple yet effective camera work, and the melody of an old song. In a way, it's a shame that this would prove to Christiane's last acting role, but on the plus side she got to become "the world's most entertained woman" as wife to Stanley Kubrick until his death in 1999, and a brilliant painter in her own right. Still, if you're only going to have one role in a movie, Paths of Glory is a pretty good choice.

Paths of Glory is so rich and layered that it seems to get better with each viewing and every passing year. They may be able to replicate the look of war on screen with expensive special effects and CGI nowadays, but they can't truly capture the feel of it, and the gut wrenching fear of conflict like Stanley Kubrick could.

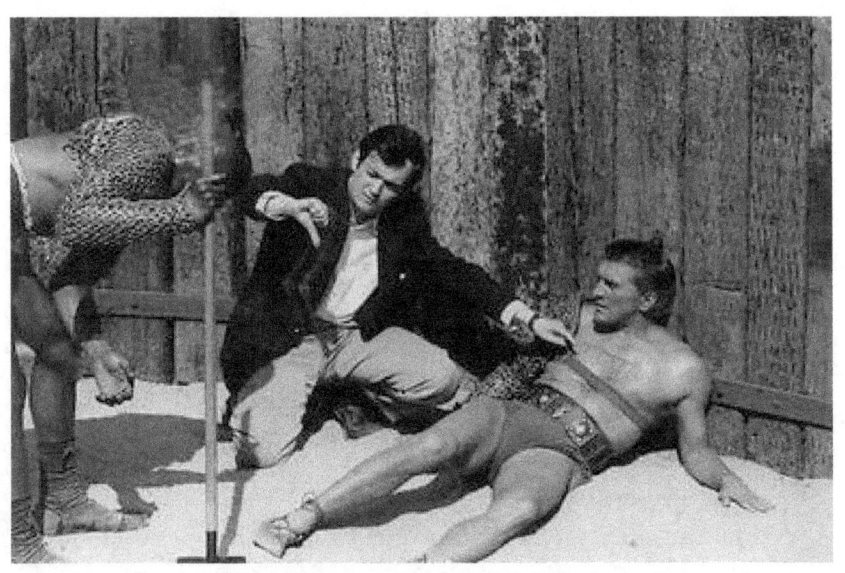

SPARTACUS (1960)

"He'll be a fine director some day. If he falls flat on his face just once. It might teach him how to compromise."

\- Kirk Douglas on Kubrick, 1960

Spartacus is the one film which sticks out in Kubrick's filmography as being totally uncharacteristic of his work. Sure, Spartacus is a great studio picture - one of the great epics of the fifties and sixties no less - but it was a "job" for Stanley, nothing more, and there was very little, possibly no room at all for genuine personal input. Even though his previous films had come from pre-existing text, they were still his sole directorial vision and he was very much in the driving seat for these adaptations. Spartacus, though, was something different all together, an experience he didn't enjoy, but one he undoubtedly learned a lot from.

In truth, the period of time in the wake of Paths of Glory was a strange and strained phase for Stanley. For six months he worked with Marlon Brando on a script for a western, and though a major chunk of his time was taken up by the project, it came to nothing. Soon after, in February 1959, Stanley got a call from Kirk Douglas, who had starred in his previous picture, with a very tempting offer on the set of Spartacus. The film's original director Anthony Mann had been fired by Douglas early on in production, and Kubrick was offered 150,000 dollars to take over. Needing the money and with no other projects in sight, Kubrick accepted the deal.

"Yes, its the only picture I've worked on where I was employed," Kubrick told Terry Southern, "and in a situation like that the director has no real rights, except the rights of persuasion... and I've found that's the wrong end of the lever to be on. First of all, you very often fail to persuade, and secondly, even when you do persuade, you waste so much time doing it that it gets to be ridiculous."

"I did two scripts that no one wanted," Kubrick explained in another interview, showing how well and truly lost he was in that period for new inspiration. "A year went by and my finances were rather rocky. I received no salary for The Killing or Paths of Glory but had worked on 100 per cent deferred salary -- and since the films didn't make any money, I had received nothing from either of them. I subsisted on loans from my partner, Jim Harris. Next I spent six months working on a screenplay for a Western, One-Eyed Jacks, with Marlon Brando and Calder Willingham. Our relationship ended amicably a few weeks before Marlon began directing the film himself. By the time I had left Brando I had spent two years doing nothing. At this point, I was hired to direct Spartacus with Kirk Douglas. It was the only one of my films over which I did not have complete control; although I was the director, mine was only one of many voices to which Kirk listened. I am disappointed in the film. It had everything but a good story."

Kubrick, often criticised for being a control freak, was merely an artist who cared passionately about what he did and put his name to. He wanted to be in charge of every aspect of a film - editing, directing, filming, sound, conceptual ideas, casting, costumes, design - but only because he was sure to get the exact results he required with such control. For him, the making of Spartacus, where he had no authority at all and was basically a hired hand, was something of an artistic nightmare; one he got nothing out of, except a good pay cheque. Though it looked good on his CV, and was a sizeable success, it was not an experience he was going to see himself in ever again.

Set during the Third Servile War, it stars Kirk Douglas as the hero of the title, who leads a rebellion against the Romans. At three hours long and with a 12 million budget, it was a gloriously overblown Hollywood production, with a whole cast of superstars, like Tony Curtis, Laurence Olivier and Charles Laughton. Anthony Mann, famed for such western classics as Winchester '73, was the initial director but was fired by Kirk over production disagreements. Anyone else would have been daunted and out of their comfort zone, especially a relative newcomer like Kubrick. But this was Stanley, not just any director. And though there weren't many films behind him at that point, he had become an expert in various areas of filmmaking. He had already proved he could handle small gatherings of contemporary people in his earlier projects, and had also proved himself quite the master of capturing the hellish realism of war. The battle scenes in Paths of Glory alone were enough to warrant the direction over such a massively scaled project, but no one really knew how he would fare with a huge epic like Spartacus. As it turned out, he took to it naturally, though he was still very much following orders and doing whatever his star desired him to do. Kubrick was surprisingly grounded considering it was such an overwhelming situation, but understanding his meagre role in the situation, he was able to compartmentalise his misgivings about the production and get on with fulfilling his role.

Spartacus's scale is unquestionably huge, but despite the juxtaposition from his earlier, smaller budgeted films, Kubrick could see the similarities between big and small productions. "The making of any film, whatever the historical setting or the size of the sets, has to be approached in much the same way," he later said. "You have to figure out what is going on in each scene and what's the most interesting way to play it. With Spartacus, whether a scene had hundreds of people in the background or whether it was against a wall, I thought of everything first as if there was nothing back there. Once it was rehearsed, we worked out the background. When Spartacus was being made, I discussed this point with Olivier and Ustinov and they both said that they felt that their powers were just drifting off into space when they were working out of doors. Their minds weren't sharp and their concentration seemed to evaporate. They preferred that kind of focusing-in that happens in a studio with the lights pointing at them and the sets around them. Whereas outside everything fades away, inside there is a kind of inner focusing of physical energy."

While Kubrick was never truly satisfied with the film, it does contains sequences which can sit proudly in the inevitable classic Kubrick montage which will last through history. And even if you don't really count it as a true Kubrick movie, it's an essential step in his development. By the end of production, and when he was on to his next film project (which turned out to be Lolita, no less), Kubrick was already playing down his association with the picture. Spartacus, a big budget Hollywood epic, was the kind of film he had viewed dead eyed back in New York when frequenting the local cinema, and was of the same breed of picture that had inspired him to make movies of his own; not because he was inspired by the content of your standard Hollywood schlock of course, but because he was challenged, egged on if you like, by the fact that he couldn't possibly make a film as bad as that. Speaking just after the release of Spartacus, New York Times reported in as many words that Stanley was itching to get on with his next movie, one which would impress the avant-garde buffs. The "costume epics" are openly frowned upon in the piece, which is concluded with Kubrick himself stating, "Let's say, that I was more influenced by Eisenstein's Alexander Nevsky than by Ben Hur or anything by Cecil .B. De Mille."

As much as he wanted to sneer at the film though, it did massive business, received multiple Oscars, got some good notices, a lot of exposure and is now very much a classic. While it contains no real sign of the Kubrick trademark, and is often glossed over in his retrospectives - not even included in certain boxed sets in fact - it's a perversity that such a landmark production is side lined. Still,

Kubrick as the famous visionary was not present during the creation of this blockbusting mega hit, a film for the eyes, not for the mind.

Many reviewers were only lightly impressed, with New York Times at the time writing, "It is a spotty, uneven drama in which the entire opening phase representing the basic-training program in a gladiatorial school is lively, exciting and expressive, no matter how true to history it is, and the middle phase is pretentious and tedious, because it is concerned with the dull strife of politics."

Retrospective reviews have been much better. Roger Ebert gave it 3 out of 4 for its 1991 re-release, stating, "Seen three decades later in a lovingly restored version, Spartacus still plays like an extraordinary epic, and its intellectual strength is still there. But other elements of the film have dated. The most courageous thing about it, from today's standards, is that it closes without an obligatory happy ending, and an audience that has watched for 187 minutes doesn't get a tidy, mindless conclusion. The movie is about revolution, and clearly reflects the decadence of the parasitical upper classes and the superior moral fibre of the slaves. But at the end, Spartacus, like Jesus, dies on the cross. In the final scene, his wife stands beneath him and holds up their child, saying 'He will live as a free man, Spartacus.' Yes, but the baby's freedom was granted him not as its right, but because of the benevolence of the soft-hearted old Gracchus. Today, that wouldn't be good enough."

Though a classic, and one you're bound to see repeatedly on Christmas and Easter TV screenings, Spartacus is one to watch for sheer visual thrills alone; its sets, battles and showdowns, not for the plot and certainly not the dialogue. In this respect, Kubrick did a fine job. As he had no control at all over its script, his job was to ensure it looked good - and look good it certainly does. The battles are awe inspiring, as are the mass gatherings of sweeping extras and sky high sets. Though there are some good efforts (Charles Laughton in particular shines, as you'd expect), it does feel ever so clumsy in the acting stakes, as if many of the leading cast members are slightly uncomfortable in their garments and armour, delivering the clumsy dialogue. Douglas himself though gives a fine effort, carrying the picture as he had in Kubrick's previous picture, Paths of Glory.

Like Ben Hur and Cleopatra, Spartacus represents the better aspects of that great historical epic revival that came and went so fast in the fifties and sixties, before the emergence of indie cinema and the New Hollywood generation. Today, such a mammoth film would require a lot of CGI, a neater ending and actors performing rigidly before a blue screen. Nearly sixty years on, Kubrick's epic is both timeless and of its time, and wonderfully so, it has to be said.

LOLITA (1962)

"The reason I am making Lolita," Kubrick was quoted in a 1960 article in Insider's News, "is because I consider it to be a masterpiece. It would be hypocrisy for me to pretend that I am unaware of the notoriety of the book, but I am not allowing that in any way to corrupt the intention behind the making of the film. I have absolutely no misgivings about it. I think it is a perfectly suitable subject of entertainment. It is a great love story."

If Kubrick ever thought that Lolita was going to be widely accepted as a savoury love story and not cause ripples of controversy all over the world, then he was either very open minded or kidding himself. Kubrick knew damn well what Lolita was really about and how it would affect the average moviegoer, and the morally lecturing do gooders out there. In 1962, making a film about a middle aged man falling in love with a 12 year old girl was exceptionally shocking. Admittedly, it would probably cause even more upset and outrage today in a post feminist world where we are more conscious and carefully aware of the problems surrounding such subject matter. Against all odds, Kubrick was intent on making the film; but then he wasn't your average director in it for the bucks, the fame and the arse kissing. He was an artist who happened to be working in the medium of film, a man who felt a desire to bring risqué issues to the fore, to discuss the lesser explored themes and provoke active thought. he was the thinking man's filmmaker.

Lolita, based on the classic novel by Vladimir Nabokov and adapted for the screen by the author himself, was Kubrick's first British production, the place he was soon to be calling his permanent home. To get the best results from the passionate script, he assembled a fine cast of seasoned veterans, and thought long and hard about getting the right face for each role. James B. Harris wanted James Mason for the part of Humbert from the word go, but Kubrick had others in mind initially. He wrote a letter to Laurence Olivier, who he had just directed in Spartacus, asking him to consider a collaboration on bringing the controversial piece to life. Kubrick sent Olivier a letter to illustrate how perfect he would be in the film, but the stage legend had reservations. A few months later, after serious consideration, Laurence Oliver's reply went thus:

Having scrutinised the book curiously and intensely during the last week I do not feel my mind grasping a film conception of the subject and I therefore don't feel that I can very well bear the onus of the responsibility of partnership in the script of a subject concerning which strong doubts are so uppermost in my mind. These doubts come from a conviction that the chief merit in the book lies in the author's brilliant original and witty descriptive powers and I can't see how this particular virtue is photographable. I fear that told in terms of dialogue the subject would be reduced to the level of pornography to which I'm afraid quite a few people already consign it.

Whether Olivier doubted the prospects of a decent film adaptation or was just afraid of the possible backlash is anyone's guess, but the big man was out of the picture. Other actors pondered upon included Peter Ustinov, another Spartacus star, and David Niven, who actually signed up for the role, but quickly withdrew his commitment.

Undoubtedly, it was the controversy which he knew the film was bound to attract that caused him to change his mind. But things worked out in the end when Mason turned down a theatre run that had initially kept him from taking on the lead in Lolita, and finally committed to the film.

"Yes, I always thought he had just the right qualities for Humbert - you know, handsome but vulnerable," Kubrick said of Mason's appeal, "sort of easy-to-hurt and also a romantic - because that was true of Humbert, of course, that beneath that veneer of sophistication and cynicism, and that sort of affected sneer, he was terribly romantic and sentimental."

The casting of Lolita herself was the most vital of all. She couldn't be too old as to appear womanly and conventionally appealing to the older man, but she couldn't look too young either, which would turn the film into a perverted affair. Sue Lyon was eventually selected, reportedly because her figure was already a little curvier than other girls her age - she was 15 when the film was shown to the public. The selection was perfect; Lyon *is* Lolita in every way. "She was actually just the right age," Kubrick said of Sue fitting snugly into the role.

As we wash the dreadful 1997 remake from our minds (one shudders at the thought of a leering Jeremy Irons in that awful update), we must embrace the sheer grace and perfection of Kubrick's updating of the novel, and its considerable taming down of what may have been a potentially unpleasant film. Today, Kubrick might have dared make it according to the original text, but in 1962, this was beyond a possibility. He would later tame down Anthony Burgess' A Clockwork Orange for the screen, for all of our blessings, as a direct book to screen adaptation would have made for an unwatchable and gruesome experience. Again, Kubrick knew very well where the parameters between good and bad taste lie, and with Lolita he managed to skirt healthily over the edge of it, just enough to ensure his film was talked about in hushed reverence.

Still, Stanley felt held back by the times. He explained this in one interview, stating, "I would fault myself in one area of the film, however; because of all the pressure over the Production Code and the Catholic Legion of Decency at the time, I believe I didn't sufficiently dramatize the erotic aspect of Humbert's relationship with Lolita, and because his sexual obsession was only barely hinted at, many people guessed too quickly that Humbert was in love with Lolita. Whereas in the novel this comes as a discovery at the end, when she is no longer a nymphet but a dowdy, pregnant suburban housewife; and it's this encounter, and his sudden realization of his love, that is one of the most poignant elements of the story. If I could do the film over again, I would have stressed the erotic component of their relationship with the same weight Nabokov did. But that is the only major area where I believe the film is susceptible to valid criticism."

Of course, much of the subtlety is what makes the film more effective, and Kubrick still gets to the core of the matter without explicit imagery. He playfully glides around the edges of decency and avoids the crippling brunt of censorship, turning the film into a more imaginative, metaphorical study of forbidden infatuation. There are certain scenes which were shocking at the time, but look tame by today's standards. Still, by being clever and slightly wily, Stanley was able to get to the heart of this unsavoury obsession. After all, having the opportunity to be explicit, or resort straight to explicitness, can often lead to less inspired and far lazier results. (Anyone who has seen the modern "torture porn" horror films will see they are idiotic in comparison to intelligent horror films like, for instance, Kubrick's The Shining.) In this case, Kubrick's limitations turned out to be beneficial for the film's ambiguity.

Subject matter aside, the film looks simply beautiful, the black and white photography lending it a touch of class despite, or perhaps because of the subject matter. Had Lolita been presented to us in full colour, its artfulness may have been lost in translation. Though Kubrick is the true star here, the acting is tremendous, with James Mason more animated than usual and perfect as the bewitched Humbert. Shelley Winters is brilliantly fiery as his wife, and Sue Lyon herself is fantastic, a revelation in fact, and it's a shame that her career never took off afterwards, despite her bagging a Golden Globe for the movie.

The finest acting work for me though comes from Peter Sellers in the quirky role of Quilty, his first of two screen collaborations with Stanley. Utterly hilarious in a dark and slightly nightmarish manner, as magnetic as ever on screen, Sellers the shape shifter puts in one of his most iconic and memorable film performances.

In hindsight, it's a thought provoking study of midlife crisis, a misguided crush that grows more intense as the movie goes on. So it's easy to overlook the storm of criticism Lolita received at the time, and it did indeed suffer a great backlash. Despite this, or perhaps due to this, it performed well at the box office, making back five times its budget.

"It must be said that Mr. Kubrick has got a lot of fun and frolic in his film," New York Times wrote in one of the kindest reviews for the time. "He has also got a bit of pathos and irony toward the end. Unfortunately, there are some strange confusions of style and mood as it moves along. The changes are disconcerting, and Mr. Kubrick inclines to dwell too long over scenes that have slight purpose, such as scenes in which Mr. Sellers does various comical impersonations as the sneaky villain who dogs Mr. Mason's trail. But, for all that, the picture has a rare power, a garbled but often moving push toward an off-beat communication. And Miss Lyon makes a shallow, heartless girl. This is not the novel Lolita, but it is a provocative sort of film."

"The result is an occasionally amusing but shapeless film about a middle aged professor who comes to no good end through his involvement with a well-developed teenager," Variety reported. "The fact that the first third of the picture is so good, bristling with Nabokovisms – a gun, for example, referred to as a tragic treasure – underscores the final disappointment. There is much about the film that is excellent. James Mason has never been better than he is as erudite Humbert Humbert, driven by a furious passion for a rather slovenly, perverse 'nymphet' (a term, incidentally, which is used only once in the entire film). He is especially good in the early sequences as he pursues Lolita to the point where he even marries her mother, whom Shelley Winters plays to bumptious perfection."

Today, Lolita is rightfully seen as an influential and hugely important work, sitting at the start of a revolutionary decade which managed to surpass all limitations and boundaries. Had Kubrick and his contemporaries known that redefining the lines of acceptance would result in some of the dross that is churned out these days - largely films with no meaning or message, just guts, nudity and garish special effects - one argues they may have pondered whether it was even worth it, for the future of cinema as we know it.

DR STRANGELOVE (1964)

"What we are dealing with is film by fiat, film by frenzy."
- Stanley Kubrick on the set of Dr Strangelove

Though he toyed with humour in other films, and drew laughs in darker corners with the likes of A Clockwork Orange, Dr Strangelove is the only true comedy in the Kubrick canon. Malcolm McDowell has noted that during the creation of the final hospital scene in A Clockwork Orange, Kubrick would be on the floor, tissues shoved into his mouth, laughing hysterically at Malcolm's antics. Kubrick and McDowell thought they were making a dark comedy, and were utterly surprised at the backlash of outrage the film received. Seven years earlier though, there was no doubt that Dr Strangelove, subtitled How I Learned to Stop Worrying and Love the Bomb, was an all out comedy, albeit one with its finger on the pulse of the times. A complete ripping apart of the Cold War and the paranoiac state of the USA against the spread of communism, and its fear of the Soviet Union, Dr Strangelove was met with equal measures of delight and shock. Like with all Kubrick's films, it took time for wide spread acclaim to come its way.

Now looked back upon as one of the finest comedies of all time, Kubrick had a hard time in getting people to understand his vision of the novel Red Alert by Peter George. Adapted from the book by Kubrick and Terry Southern, with help from the author, it poked fun at the fears of a nuclear war, the end of days, the man made apocalypse that was undoubtedly around the corner. Fifty odd years on and we're still here... for now at least. The current looming threat of devastation, and the madness of the Trump government, ensure us that Dr Strangelove is more relevant than ever, and we may witness a resurgence of interest in the film from a new generation of disillusioned, world weary lost souls, trying to figure out what's happened to us.

Back in the early sixties though, it was a story Kubrick had searched hard for, and one he had fallen in love with. Another co-production between the US and the UK, Kubrick took the project with all his usual enthusiasm and attention to detail. However, it wasn't initially supposed to be a comedy at all.

"I started work on the screenplay with every intention of making the film a serious treatment of the problem of accidental nuclear war," Kubrick revealed. "As I kept trying to imagine the way in which things would really happen, ideas kept coming to me which I would discard because they were so ludicrous. I kept saying to myself: I can't do this. People will laugh. But after a month or so I began to realize that all the things I was throwing out were the things which were most truthful. After all, what could be more absurd than the very idea of two mega-powers willing to wipe out all human life because of an accident, spiced up by political differences that will seem as meaningless to people a hundred years from now as the theological conflicts of the Middle Ages appear to us today? So it occurred to me that I was approaching the project in the wrong way. The only way to tell the story was as a black comedy or, better, a nightmare comedy, where the things you laugh at most are really the heart of the paradoxical postures that make a nuclear war possible. "

Kubrick saw his characters in Strangelove like any others, as people reacting to ludicrous but not entirely unrealistic situations. "Most of the humour in Strangelove arises from the depiction of everyday human behaviour in a nightmarish situation," he claimed, "like the Russian premier on the hot line who forgets the telephone number of his general staff headquarters and suggests the American President try Omsk information, or the reluctance of a U.S. officer to let a British officer smash open a Coca-Cola machine for change to phone the President about a crisis on the SAC base because of his conditioning about the sanctity of private property."

Dr Strangelove was a good chance for Kubrick to work with one of his favourite comedy actors again, Peter Sellers, who showed his true comedic genius by taking on three roles; Captain Mandrake, President Muffley and Dr Strangelove himself. Possibly Sellers' crowning cinematic moment, it's his chance to truly shine, to let loose, and to run pretty much free under Kubrick's supervision. It's the Goons Show brought to the silver screen. The characters are so varied and vivid that were you not aware of Sellers' shape shifting, chameleon-like talents, you would easily believe these were three separate individuals. On his inspiration for the eye patch wearing, wheel chair bound former Nazi science mastermind Strangelove, Sellers set the record straight: "Strangelove was never modelled after Kissinger - that's a popular misconception. It was always Wernher Von Braun." Von Braun was a Nazi rocket scientist, who went on to serve for America after the end of the Second World War, and eventually became a born again Evangelical Christian. There's a Kubrick film in that life story for sure.

"When Peter arrived on the set he usually arrived walking very slowly and staring morosely," Kubrick said. "I'd clear the crew from the stage and we'd begin rehearsing. As the work progressed, he would respond to something in the scene, his mood would visibly brighten, and we would begin to have fun. Improvisational ideas began to click. On many occasions I believe Peter reached a comic ecstasy. I filmed him with many cameras, never less than three."

It's very much the Peter Sellers show, and for anyone who's a fan of his varied skill with multiple characters and voices, it's a treat from start to finish. Though temperamental and troubled, Kubrick was able to find ways to make it work with the actor. And thank god, for without Sellers, what would Dr Strangelove have been? Perhaps a more straight faced and valid adaptation of Red Alert, but definitely nothing on this hilarious scale.

Kubrick toyed with various titles, like Dr Doomsday and Wonderful Bomb, before deciding on Dr Strangelove with Southern, who Kubrick had brought in for co writing after enjoying his novel, The Magic Christian. Filmed at Shepperton Studios near London, it was the beginning of Stanley's home grown ethic, where in making a film he didn't have to travel too many miles out of his comfort zone. The movies came to him, not the other way round.

Dr Strangelove is not only a great comedy, it's also a masterpiece of visuals and set design. Without the dazzling, stark and often frighteningly imposing sets of legendary film designer Ken Adam, the film would have lost some of its weight. The War Room alone, copied hundreds of times in subsequent movies, is enough to put the film in legend, and its gathering of various mad men and eccentrics brings to mind the underground lair of Dr Evil in Mike Myer's

70

wonderful Austin Powers movies, which beyond a shadow of a doubt were influenced by Strangelove.

Getting an insider's view of the awe inspiring settings, co-writer Terry Southern reported on set for Esquire: "The War Room at Shepperton Studios outside London is one of the largest indoor sets ever built. It is 130 feet long and 100 feet wide, with a 35-foot high ceiling. The walls are made of huge electronic world-target maps which cast back in weird reflection from the high-gloss black floor. The mammoth circular table, seating the Prez and his council, is covered with green baize, like a monstrous gaming-table, and is 380 square feet in surface area."

This was Kubrick's first large scale personal film, and is a landmark for him in every way. Every shot is masterfully executed; people and objects exactly where they should be; lighting, shadows and mood are consistent throughout the film's duration; the performances are wild but constrained, feral yet controlled. By getting the right people for the right roles, particularly Sellers, and entrusting them with the script, Kubrick ensured Strangelove was his most eccentric and daring film up to that point. Lolita had featured a great deal of the Kubrick stamp, all classy shots and provocative twists of conventions, but Strangelove is simply on another level. Consider the scenes of Sellers as Strangelove, fighting back his Nazi salute; the amazing, much copied scene of the man riding the nuclear bomb as it comes rocketing to the ground; the sequence where Vera Lynn (Note: it's her 100th birthday as I write this piece) sings "We'll meet again.. don't know where, don't know when" as nuclear clouds spread out across the land. For the first time, the Kubrick brain had been fully projected out on to the screen, without censorship, and the results were undeniably wonderful.

Beneath the laughs though, is one of Kubrick's most clear and concise statements. The farcical setting is merely a mask for poking at the comical attitudes of the Cold War. The perfectly abbreviated MAD (Mutual Assured Destruction) is used to highlight the sheer ridiculousness of the spat, men acting like children while their fingers hover over the button which could destroy us all. By keeping each other in check, a kind of chaotic order is assumed. As a former chess champion, the irony of this may not have been lost on Kubrick. Chess is a recurring idea in his subsequent films, and some have argued that each movie is paced and pieced together like the complex game of wits; the idea of time running out, characters enclosing on others, the mind games. Though one can tire of certain metaphorical theorising on cinema, the Kubrick chess idea is a valid one. The brain of a chess player will undoubtedly be sharper, more logical and mathematic. Whether Kubrick really did have an IQ of 200 or not, it's clear by the way his films are constructed that there was a lot more going on in his mind than others.

Kubrick himself would explain how chess can relate to life itself, and by life, he clearly meant the movies, which *were* his life. "Among a great many other things that chess teaches you is to control the initial excitement you feel when you see something that looks good," he explained to Playboy in 1968. "It trains you to think before grabbing, and to think just as objectively when you're in trouble."

A reporter by the name of Jeremy Bernstein was one of the only media men Kubrick seemed to warm to. Why? Was it due to his sympathetic articles on Kubrick, or was it his love for chess? A writer for the New Yorker, he began visiting Kubrick during the making of 2001, and when he did so, he would play chess with Kubrick between takes. On the set of Dr Strangelove, Stanley famously played chess with George C Scott. This paints a portrait of a man who was 100 percent switched on during film preparation, 100 percent switched on during takes, and 100 percent switched on during breaks in filming. His mind, essentially, never stopped working.

Reviews for Dr Strangelove were memorable to say the least, and it was clear by many of the notices that Kubrick had arrived as a name in his own right, a man building his own cinematic sub-universe separate from the mainstream Hollywood machine of predictability. "Producer director Stanley Kubrick has with skill and daring," raved Variety, "fashioned a sharply satirical comedy on a subject as sensitive as Top Security – a nuclear holocaust – in the Columbia Picture release, Dr. Strangelove... Nothing would seen to be farther apart than nuclear war and comedy, yet Kubrick's caper eloquently tackles a Fail-Safe subject with a light touch. While there are times when it hurts to laugh because somehow there is a feeling that the mad events in Strangelove could happen, it emerges as a most unusual combination of comedy and suspense. Kubrick also directed the film by his own production company, and successfully captured the incongruous elements of Strangelove with a deft, professional touch. It would seem no setting for comedy or satire, but the writers have accomplished this with biting, piercing dialogue and thorough characterizations."

Retrospectively, it's become one of Kubrick's most acclaimed films. While some of his later masterpieces like Full Metal Jacket, The Shining and Eyes Wide Shut have their own cult followings, their apparent "flaws" are often pointed out, and they still serve as firm favourites despite their supposed shortcomings. Dr Strangelove though, seems to attract very little if any negativity from critics and film historians. All these years on, the satire still works, savagely so, and the ideas are more eerily close to home. Writing in 1999, Roger Ebert called it the best satire of the century, and you would have to ponder for a while to find a match for it. They couldn't make another one like it, that's for sure.

In a piece for Newsweek in 1964, Kubrick would be more telling about Strangelove than ever. "The greatest message of the film is in the laughs," he said with clarity. "You know, it's true! The most realistic things are the funniest." At the end of the piece, he flirts with the concept of 2001, and claims to have got to grips with storytelling on screen. He mentions his fascination with outer space, and also adds, "I'm now interested in taking a story, fantastic and improbable, and trying to get to the bottom of it, to make it seem not only real, but inevitable. I can always do a story about overpopulation. Do you realize that in 2020 there will be no room on earth for all the people to stand? The really sophisticated worriers are worried about that."

Always a worrier, that Stanley Kubrick. Wonder what he'd make of the Trump government?

2001: A SPACE ODYSSEY (1968)

"If anyone understands it on the first viewing,
we've failed in our intention."
- Arthur C Clarke on 2001

And so, just like that, Stanley Kubrick invented a new genre, something he himself called a "mythical documentary." The film was a long time coming, for the very logical, precise and ultra intellectual Kubrick was forever fascinated by the idea of life existing on other planets. He very much desired to explore the possibility of extra terrestrial life, the mysterious enigma of space on the silver screen - but he wanted to do it right. Advised by a friend to collaborate with a specific figure who could help bring his ideas to life, Kubrick got in touch with sci-fi icon Arthur C Clarke. The wonderful letter he sent to Clarke is very open, heartily respectful and well worth reprinting here. There are little signs of the supposedly difficult man others professed him to be.:

Dear Mr Clarke:

It's a very interesting coincidence that our mutual friend Caras mentioned you in a conversation we were having about a Questar telescope. I had been a great admirer of your books for quite a time and had always wanted to discuss with you the possibility of doing the proverbial "really good" science-fiction movie.

My main interest lies along these broad areas, naturally assuming great plot and character:

1, The reasons for believing in the existence of intelligent extra-terrestrial life.

2, The impact (and perhaps even lack of impact in some quarters) such discovery would have on Earth in the near future.

3, A space probe with a landing and exploration of the Moon and Mars.

Roger [Caras] tells me you are planning to come to New York this summer. Do you have an inflexible schedule? If not, would you consider coming sooner with a view to a meeting, the purpose of which would be to determine whether an idea might exist or arise which could sufficiently interest both of us enough to want to collaborate on a screenplay?

Incidentally, "Sky & Telescope" advertise a number of scopes. If one has the room for a medium size scope on a pedestal, say the size of a camera tripod, is there any particular model in a class by itself, as the Questar is for small portable scopes?

Best regards

The respect was mutual. Clarke and Kubrick proved to be the perfect pair to bring man's curious pondering on the ever expanding universe to the big screen. It was a huge departure from his last film though, the comedic and heavily satirical Dr. Strangelove, and the approach wouldn't be so much as different, but coming from another galaxy all together.

"Strangelove was a film where much of its impact hinged on the dialogue, the mode of expression, the euphemisms employed," Stanley said in 1969, comparing 2001 to Dr Strangelove. "As a result, it's a picture that is largely destroyed in translation or dubbing. 2001, on the other hand, is basically a visual, nonverbal experience. It avoids intellectual verbalization and reaches the viewer's subconscious in a way that is essentially poetic and philosophic. The film thus becomes a subjective experience which hits the viewer at an inner level of consciousness, just as music does, or painting."

"2001 is a nonverbal experience," he said in another interview, "out of two hours and 19 minutes of film, there are only a little less than 40 minutes of dialog. I tried to create a visual experience, one that bypasses verbalized pigeonholing and directly penetrates the subconscious with an emotional and philosophic content."

Like many of Kubrick's films, it's a grower for sure. When I first watched it as a late teen hung up on A Clockwork Orange, I have to admit that in my lack of depth I found it tedious. Silly I know, given the wonderment of the visuals. But being born in the 1980s, I grew up in a time when visual effects were used ad nauseam, and by the late 90s were dominating over all aspects of story and cinematic taste. Effects then, were not what I was after. I was done with them. I wanted plot, dialogue and characters; 2001 had none of this, which my straight forward thinking at the time could not comprehend. When I started to mature, I began to enjoy it more and more, admiring its beauty and daring scope. By my late twenties, I viewed it like most sensible folk as a masterpiece. As with a lot of Stanley's work, you grow fonder as time goes on and as you develop as a human being. After all, we all begin our lives like the apes at the start of 2001, and some of us who are lucky enough might just advance a little beyond that.

From its iconic opening sequence, 2001 is a film that highlights the importance of imagery in film; or more to the point, well directed imagery in film. At the time of release, science fiction hadn't been handled on an intellectual level and no film of its genre had put you right into space, or wholly pondered the issues of space travel, extra terrestrial life and the darkness beyond. Firstly exploring man's infancy in the simplistic prehistoric ape world of long ago, 2001 goes on to tackle the battle between man and machine, a battle that never really seems like a war, but more of a subtle, slow motion take over. It is a film that looks at the advancement of technology and the emotional downfall of the emotional man as a result of this. Like Strangelove before it, and in an age of tablets, mobile phones, Facebook and so called "social media", it's more relevant than ever.

The opening section, Dawn of Man, is by far my personal favourite part of the film. The mysterious atmosphere transports you to another time and eerily conveys the mood of a human-free landscape. Kubrick has his stamp all over the early part of the film, with his revolutionary use of music on the soundtrack, alongside the grunting sounds of primitive communication. The booming sounds of Strauss give the scene its real punch, and the film benefits greatly from using the music of the old masters. Though some criticised Kubrick for not hiring enough composers to score fresh new works for his movies, Kubrick's decision to use the old classics was valid. If you're going to show a painting, you might as well choose the great masters of old - Da Vinci, Michelangelo etc. - over a new piece of art. For Kubrick and his way with music, the attitude was the same.

"However good our best film composers may be, they are not a Beethoven, a Mozart or a Brahms," Kubrick told Michael Ciment.

"Why use music which is less good when there is such a multitude of great orchestral music available from the past and from our own time? When you are editing a film, it's very helpful to be able to try out different pieces of music to see how they work with the scene... Well, with a little more care and thought, these temporary tracks can become the final score."

I find it hard to fathom how I ever had a problem with 2001, but to highlight how a film can reveal its glories to you over repeated viewings, and how understanding comes with only a few more years on this earth, here is a segment from a review I wrote on the film for Hound Dawg Magazine in 2011:

"The second part (of the film) is where I understand people's criticisms with it being slow. While it was great to see Leonard Rossitier (one of my favourite actors), I could not be fully engaged by anything in this section of the film, that is when the characters were speaking. Clearly, the film only slightly grabs me when it's mixing amazing images with amazing music. But maybe I missed the point; the tiny men and women are insignificant in comparison to the sheer importance of the space craft and this film is not a look at human development. It studies man's emotional decline and the machine's rise. Kubrick explores the craft's movements as if the objects themselves are pieces of art; or more to the point, like pieces of sublime music. You must remember visuals like this were unseen at the time, yet Kubrick's slow take on the beauty looks a little over the top today. The film is about technology, and the gradual advancement of that. Without proper engaging characters and plot though, I struggled to be fully engaged and interested. Or is it just me? Hal, the ship's computer in the third part of the film, and the

chilling prospects he offers us in an ever advancing technological world gave the film my favourite message, but it is such a disjointed, awkward film that even Hal couldn't save it for me. Visually and sonically though it is a treat, rather like a moving art gallery that offers us a realistic look at the beauty of space."

It's a rather embarrassing review, but it's essential in illustrating how ones' view of a film can totally transform. Today, I am dazzled still by almost every moment of the film, stunned by the combination of soundtrack and visuals, and totally in awe of Kubrick's reinvention of science fiction cinema. The "mythological documentary" is not something that others attempted to make, and perhaps they were wise in staying clear, for no film dealing with the enigma of eternity, space travel, alien life form and technological advancements has ever come close to it. Nearly fifty years on, after man has landed on the moon, countless space missions have been launched, Star Wars took the world by storm and the CGI revolution (or devolution?) changed film itself, 2001 remains unique, beautiful, inspiring, and despite the lack of any human feelings, very moving.

Kubrick saw 2001 as a movie to be shared and enjoyed by everyone, a film explaining itself through visuals, not dialogue or intellectual ideas, and he was keen to explain this in interviews. "I think one of the areas where 2001 succeeds is in stimulating thoughts about man's destiny and role in the universe in the minds of people who in the normal course of their lives would never have considered such matters," Kubrick said at the time. "Here again, you've got the resemblance to music; an Alabama truck driver, whose views in every other respect would be extremely narrow, is able to listen to a Beatles record on the same level of appreciation and perception as a young

Cambridge intellectual, because their emotions and subconscious are far more similar than their intellects. The common bond is their subconscious emotional reaction; and I think that a film which can communicate on this level can have a more profound spectrum of impact than any form of traditional verbal communication."

It was on the set of 2001 that Kubrick began a working relationship with one of the most significant figures in his professional life, Anthony Frewin, who became his assistant on various projects over the years. I asked Mr Frewin how he got to work with him. "Through my father who was working for Stanley at the MGM Studios. Stanley Kubrick had more confidence in me than I had in myself. I guess he saw some useful potential there." Though some of the tasks Frewin acted out for Kubrick may seem to some completely trivial and precise to the point of being unhealthy, in the context of the bigger picture they all made sense. When I asked Frewin how long it took him to get used to the tiny details Kubrick craved on 2001, he replied quite simply, "It started on day one. Working for Stanley was an on-going education."

The attention to every detail paid off though, particularly in the opening section. In lesser hands, this might have come out comedic. With Kubrick however, it came to pure perfection. "We spent an entire year trying to figure out how to make the ape-heads look convincing, and not just like a conventional makeup job," Stanley said. "We finally constructed an entire sub-skull of extremely light and flexible plastic, to which we attached the equivalent of face muscles which pulled the lips back in a normal manner whenever the mouth was opened. The mouth itself took a great deal of work -- it had artificial teeth and an artificial tongue which the actors could manipulate with tiny toggles to make the lips snarl in a lifelike fashion. Some of the masks even had built-in devices whereby the artificial muscles in the cheeks and beneath the eyes could be moved. All the apes except for two baby chimps were men, and most of them were dancers or mimes, which enabled them to move a little better than most movie apes."

The acclaimed mime artist and actor Dan Richter was Kubrick's only real choice for the ape man. I spoke to him for this book about his experiences with Kubrick.

"I first met Stanley in the fall of 1967 at his office at the MGM Studios in Borehamwood just north of London," Dan said. "He was very friendly and inquisitive with an obvious sense of humour. He had a problem with how to do the opening of the picture and wanted to know how a mime would approach it. We talked about how important it was to deal with it as an acting problem so as to immediately involve the audience. I told him that with my training as in American Mime I could approach the development of the movement as an extension of the acting process and proceeded to give him a demo of how I would do it, which he liked, and he then asked me to work with him on it. I had a great relationship with Stanley. I spent over a year working with him every day and we became good friends."

The first day on set for Dan was a memorable experience. "Because I had been developing the movement and character of Moonwatcher for 7 or 8 months it was easy for me to play him," Dan says. "Stanley always let me try things out, and while he was generally quite specific as to what he wanted, he always expected his actors to bring something to the part, and not only was open to my input regarding playing the scene, but expected it."

What was it like to be directed by a giant such as Stanley? "First of all, it was a blast to be directed by someone I considered the greatest living director," Dan told me. "I found it an easy and collaborative process of mutual discovery. He would usually do many takes as he liked to feel his way into a shot and as the takes progressed he would incorporate what he had discovered from the prior ones. It was about six to eight weeks."

Dan also told me an amusing story about Stanley and a habit he had. "Christiane, Stanley's wife, did not want him to smoke so he didn't carry cigarettes, so every time we saw each other he would cage a cigarette from me. Perhaps what I loved most was that while we were always talking about the picture we were also talking about endless other subjects that interested us."

"I didn't go to the opening in the States," Dan told me, "so I was at the London premiere. It was hard for me to watch because I was being critical of my section, and I had seen so much of the rest of the picture during the time we were developing it. It's always hard for me to watch something I'm in as there is no magic. I've seen it quite a few times in recent years and it's much easier for me to watch. I am honored to be part of such a masterpiece."

I asked Dan if he ever saw Kubrick again after filming was over. "Only a few times. I went over to his house during the making of A Clockwork Orange to loan him an editing table that I had had built for John and Yoko Lennon (Note: Dan worked as an assistant to John and Yoko after 2001). Shortly after I returned to the States and we were on different sides of the ocean until he died."

The film is a complete and utter classic now, but at the time it was met with some serious criticism. Of course, this was to be expected from the somewhat "caveman" mentality of old Hollywood, so it was thankful when 2001 was officially adopted by the counterculture as something of a psychedelic freak out movie. It was a huge hit, making over 100 million dollars at the box office.

Variety were critical, and slightly ludicrous too, writing, "Stanley Kubrick is alive and well and living in Outer Space. Those filmgoers who have wondered what happened to the man who gave screen birth to Lolita and Dr. Strangelove can stop worrying. He's taken up a new hobby – science-fiction – and his first effort comes close to running away with itself. One criticism that will be raised is that film cost too much for so "personal" (i.e. Kubrick) a film. The commercial future of 2001 will be followed with interest. With an initial print order of 103, Metro evidently intends to follow up its Washington (Tues.) and New York (Wed.) premieres with numerous openings, as suggested by the tremendous promotional campaign on the film already underway. But 2001 is not a cinematic landmark. It compares with, but does not best, previous efforts at science fiction; lacking the humanity of Forbidden Planet, the imagination of Things to Come and the simplicity of Of Stars and Men, it actually belongs to the technically-slick group previously dominated by George Pal and the Japanese."

The New York Times were even more vocal in their distaste, writing, "The movie is so completely absorbed in its own problems, its use of colour and space, its fanatical devotion to science-fiction detail, that it is somewhere between hypnotic and immensely boring. The special effects in the movie — particularly a voyage, either through

Dullea's eye or through the slab and over the surface of Jupiter-Earth and into a period bedroom — are the best I have ever seen; and the number of ways in which the movie conveys visual information (there is very little dialogue) drives it to an outer limit of the visual. And yet the uncompromising slowness of the movie makes it hard to sit through without talking — and people on all sides when I saw it were talking almost throughout the film. Very annoying. With all its attention to detail — a kind of revelling in its own I.Q. — the movie acknowledged no obligation to validate its conclusion for those, me for example, who are not science-fiction buffs."

There is a lot of talk these days of movies being an experience, with the much overused word "awesome" rearing its head time and time again in regards to superhero schlock and third rate sci-fi romps with special effects overload and money to burn. But 2001: A Space Odyssey is a real singular experience in itself, a work of art, existing in its own parallel cinematic universe, raising questions but never answering them, probing at the mysteries out there yet never cracking the egg of wonderment. It is, though I hate to use the word, truly awesome, a cinematic journey to be truly in awe of.

A CLOCKWORK ORANGE (1971)

Where to begin when it comes to one of the most important, popular, iconic and controversial films in cinema history? Historically, A Clockwork Orange came from the most shocking era of film, where these outrageous offending articles were either condemned, banned, or for that matter, both. Along with Sam Peckinpah's Straw Dogs and Ken Russell's The Devils, A Clockwork Orange was unleashed in a time where no one had seen this kind of shocking film before. Nearly half a century on, it is still as fresh in people's minds now as it was in the early 70s. But why? Is it due to its 25 year ban in Britain, an act that only increased its inevitable myth? Is it because its dark predictions of social meltdown and chaos are ringing truer with each passing year? Or is it down to the actual film, all its memorable screen moments that have become classic, and the iconic imagery it has branded into pop culture? The very costume that McDowell wears in the film, that familiar eye lash, bowler hat, and jock strap, has being replicated in such varied fields as The Simpsons, every year on Halloween, fancy dress parties, Madonna and Kylie Minogue's large scale live shows, fashion catwalks and magazine covers. Everywhere, and often in the most unlikely of places, you will see a distinct Clockwork Orange influence. Artists such as The Addicts, Alice Cooper, Blur, Muse, Eminem, Christina Aguilera and Rob Zombie have adopted the outfit, while others like Moloko and Heaven 17 are subtly named after the milk drink and a fictitious group in the film. There are so many unforgettable images and scenes in the film itself; the tunnel where the old man is beaten, the milk bar, the rape of the writer's wife, the scene where Malcolm has lid locks on his eyes when he is forced to watch horrific videos for the Ludovico treatment. No wonder the world refuses to forget it.

In modern life, particularly among teens, there is this feeling that it is generally cool to like A Clockwork Orange, or at least say you do (even if you haven't even seen it). Some don't really take on board what the message is, or what the film has to say about society, the system and free will. But does that really matter? Has it got to the point now where the film's notoriety has surpassed the contents within it? Has it become a case of style over content? Maybe so, but it's undeniable that this is still one of the most outstanding, important and influential films of all time, sceptics' put downs aside.

The story follows 15 year old Alex (McDowell), a generally nasty but charming member of a violent youth gang who prowl the night, beating other gangs, raping "devotchkas" and drinking drug spiked milk (Moloko plus) in a strange bar. When his own gang abandon him to take the blame for a break in and murder, Alex is sent to prison. There he volunteers to take part in the testing of a new treatment being tried out on convicts, which aims to turn the bad good. He is strapped to a chair and forced to endure disturbing footage projected on a screen, all set to the back drop of his favourite music, Beethoven. The treatment succeeds in teaching him violence is bad and now at the mere thought of it, Alex is reduced to a whimpering, twitchy wreck, constantly on the verge of vomiting. When he is released he finds himself victimized by everybody, including those he previously victimized himself. The film takes a completely different turn, and Alex becomes an object of pity. Even his old gang of Droogies have become cops, and they take great delight in duffing him up real horrorshow. Alex has become a programmed robot, a victim of the system void of any opinion, in short a clockwork orange. The government is roasted by the press and political activists alike, and Alex becomes a tool in a struggle for the party's reputation. In the end, he finds himself side by side with his former opposition. "I was cured alright," he adds, right at the end of the film, sounding as evil and cocky as he did at the start.

"I first read the book about two-and-a-half years ago," Kubrick told Penelope Houston in 1971. "It was given to me by Terry Southern while I was making 2001, and due to the time pressure I was in, it joined that certain number of books that one has sitting on the shelf waiting to be read. Then one evening I passed the bookshelf, glanced at the paperback still patiently waiting on the shelf, and picked it up. I started to read the book and finished it in one sitting. By the end of Part One, it seemed pretty obvious that it might make a great film. By the end of Part Two, I was very excited about it. As soon as I finished it, I immediately reread it. For the next two or three days, I reread it in whole and in part, and did little else but think about it. It seemed to me to be a unique and marvellous work of imagination and perhaps even genius. The narrative invention was magical, the characters were bizarre and exciting, the ideas were brilliantly developed, and, equally important, the story was of a size and density that could be adapted to film without oversimplifying it or stripping it to the bones. In fact, it proved possible to retain most of the narrative in the film. Many people have praised the special language of the book, which is itself a stunning conception, but I don't think sufficient praise has been given for what might be called, for want of a better phrase, the ordinary language, which is, of course, quite extraordinary."

The underlying point is the lack of freedom of choice in modern society, Britain in this case, and it exists as a dark exploration into the state's god like control over the individual. "The central idea of the film has to do with the question of free-will," Kubrick explained to Michel Ciment in an extraordinarily frank and open interview. "Do we lose our humanity if we are deprived of the choice between good and evil? Do we become, as the title suggests, A Clockwork Orange? Recent experiments in conditioning and mind control on volunteer prisoners in America have taken this question out of the realm of science-fiction. At the same time, I think the dramatic impact of the film has principally to do with the extraordinary character of Alex, as conceived by Anthony Burgess in his brilliant and original novel. Aaron Stern, the former head of the MPAA rating board in America, who is also a practising psychiatrist, has suggested that Alex represents the unconscious: man in his *natural* state. After he is given the Ludovico 'cure' he has been 'civilized', and the sickness that follows may be viewed as the neurosis imposed by society."

In Anthony Burgess' original book, Alex chooses to be good at the end of his own accord, as opposed to the system overruling his mind in the movie. But Kubrick seems to have missed this aspect out all together; in his version, the Government puts Alex back as he was to avoid any further challenges or criticisms against their power, and as a media tool for good press. It is this very important difference which divides opinions, those who prefer Burgess' positive "good triumphs" to Kubrick's bleak, cynical, unsettling interpretation. But while dividing opinions, Kubrick also enraged Burgess, who felt his book had been ruined. To me, it's the film which has the more powerful ending, the chilling realisation that there is no free will.

This has to be up there with the most even and exciting of Kubrick's movies, although the methods of it being filmed seem rather loose by today's standards. On the set, Kubrick read from the book and they used it as a rough guide through the scenes, lifting a lot of the text for the script. The camera work is typically Kubrick, lots of steady cam and long still shots that often are so static you swear they're photos - until of course somebody moves. It gives it a realer feeling, and widens the scale of the film. The way he stages the scenes so you'll never forget them should also be applauded, with the terrific angles and strange, other worldly lighting techniques. In a lesser filmmaker's hands, this could have wound up trashy, or a very forgettable product of its time. Much of its success is down to Stanley's genius, as much as it's about Burgess' view of the world.

Again, Kubrick chose to differ from the novel he was adapting, and in this case, as with the later Shining movie, he made the text more filmic, less reliant on words alone. To Kubrick, the most important thing was still the moving image. "But my principal interest in A Clockwork Orange wasn't the language," he said, "however brilliant it was, but rather, the story, the characters and the ideas. Of course the language is a very important part of the novel, and it contributed a lot to the film, too. I think A Clockwork Orange is one of the very few books where a writer has played with syntax and introduced new words where it worked. In a film, however, I think the images, the music, the editing and the emotions of the actors are the principal tools you have to work with. Language is important but I would put it after those elements. It should even be possible to do a film which isn't gimmicky without using any dialogue at all. Unfortunately, there has been very little experimentation with the form of film stories, except in avant-garde cinema where, unfortunately, there is too little technique and expertise present to show very much. As far as I'm concerned, the most memorable scenes in the best films are those which are built predominantly of images and music."

Though set in the future, it still has a 70s look and feel to it, which is inevitable in some respects. It's here where people seem to have minor issues with the picture. Though not dated, it is very of the time it was made in, though still timeless in a more surreal way. In order to properly approach this film seriously though, you must point out what to some are the its flaws. Kevin Jackson, in a 1999 Sight and Sound article written as the film was re-released, wrote: "With Alex's induction to prison, it turns into Porridge, without Ronnie Barker's presence to humanize the poor wit." He also said, "it's a film Rik from The Young Ones would adore for its sneering attitude towards the grown up world of straights." In the almost wholly negative article he compares it to Benny Hill for its supposed obsession with tits.

This, of course, is tame criticism compared to the damning it received in the 1970s. "A painless, bloodless and pointless futuristic fantasy" said The Village Voice. "From the film comes the feeling that our children will kill us all!" wrote Alexander Walker in The Evening Standard. Among its criticism were glowing reviews too. New York Film Critics called it Film of the Year, as did New York Magazine, while Rex Reed called it "one of the most perfect films I have ever seen."

Even those who dislike the film never deny the fact that at its centre is one of the best performances in the history of cinema. As

McDowell said, it's "the role of a lifetime", and it has become the one role he is most associated with. He makes Alex menacing, violent, nasty and horrid, while in the second half he becomes funny, charming, at times pitiful and finally, a total victim. He forces the viewer to make a flip with their emotions towards him; even if you don't want to, you still end up feeling sorry for him when all the bad things start to happen. Only the most charismatic of actors could pull this off and Kubrick obviously saw this quality in McDowell when he watched him in If... It is a likability and magnetism so strong, you almost find yourself applauding his demonic acts too. As Malcolm once said himself, "Now you may not agree with what he does, but at least he enjoys it. He's not out there moping around."

There is a certain appeal to this, a kind of lust for life that is infectious, especially when indulging in some fantasy on the big screen. Seeing as Kubrick would not have made the film without McDowell, I am certain no other actor could have even pulled it off like Malcolm did. Imagine bigger names of his generation even attempting to step into Alex's shoes; it wouldn't have happened, because they would have been too worried about their reputations for sure.

Physically, Malcolm endured much pain and discomfort for the role. In the Ludovico scene his cornea was scratched by one of the lid locks holding his eyes open. He came on set with an eye patch and Stanley said, "Oh god can we shoot the other eye?" Of course the role brought him much acclaim too, with New York Film Critics, BAFTA and Golden Globe nominations.

"I had Malcolm McDowell in mind right from the third or fourth chapter of my first reading of the book," Kubrick said when the film was released, having seen and been spellbound by McDowell in Lindsay Anderson's If..., released in 1968. "One doesn't find actors of his genius in all shapes, sizes, and ages. Nor does an actor find many characters like Alex, who is certainly one of the most surprising and enjoyable inventions of fiction. I can think of only one other literary or dramatic comparison, and that is with Richard III. Alex, like Richard, is a character whom you should dislike and fear, and yet you find yourself drawn very quickly into his world and find yourself seeing things through his eyes. It's not easy to say how this is achieved, but it certainly has something to do with his candour and wit and intelligence, and the fact that all the other characters are lesser people, and in some way worse people."

Though a box office hit, it was met with a lot of criticism and negativity. But it's the passage of time which judges in the end, and A Clockwork Orange has continued to be a classic film down the years. It is, in short, a cultural phenomenon which gave birth to the punk movement and glam rock, fashion and the future of generations of film making. Everything about it to me is so perfectly done. The supporting cast are wonderfully larger than life (notably Patrick Magee as the tortured writer) and the script is just one of the most memorable ever, endlessly quotable in its humour and wit. Of course this has much to do with the Nadsat language, created by Burgess, which is a mix of Russian and fictitious words.

"Come and get one in the yarbles, if you have any yarbles, you unich jelly thou."

"Got a bit of a pain in the guliver."

"Viddy well little brother, viddy well."

Wonderful stuff.

The undeniable controversy Clockwork Orange caused within society has to be noted. Was this really a dangerous film? In Britain particularly, youths found the gang violence, here stylised and at times sensationalised, an attractive option to them, or so the press told us. The first case of supposed copycat violence was in Lancashire, as a Dutch girl on holiday was attacked by a gang in droogish costumes, all chanting "Singin' in the Rain." The film went a little further to affect the minds of the already demented, but we must put to bed the ridiculous accusations that it inspired violent behaviour from formerly decent members of society. Art as strong as Clockwork Orange cannot brainwash the innocent, but can spur on the sick and twisted. But of course Kubrick never set out to spark violence in the public; some say his movie was an essay of violence, not a step by step guide to it. Kubrick could deny the headlines for a while ("Clockwork Orange made me do it." and "The Clockwork Killer" are two well known newspaper headlines) but when the trouble turned to personal death threats addressed to him at his home, he had to do something drastic. He had it withdrawn, but only in the UK, the country he had retreated to. It remained banned until the director's death in 1999. Of course the controversy continued; even as late as 2002 a man from Hull was jailed for two murders, both his girlfriends 13 years apart. "He was obsessed with Clockwork Orange," True Crime magazine said of the killer, Peter Foster. "His first wife told the court her husband was obsessed with the film. He regularly punched her, hit her with rice flails and stabbed her with a sharpened umbrella. He often dressed in a bowler hat and wore braces like McDowell in the film. Listening to Beethoven's Ninth Symphony sent him into violent rages." No one involved with the film can be blamed for such monstrous reactions, and it is a deep shame, a tragedy in fact, that sick people can cause a work of art to be damned like A Clockwork Orange was.

"It's not so violent really," Malcolm said retrospectively. "It was tamed down from the book." He has also spoken of how modern audiences pick up on things that the 70s audience didn't, especially the humour. "I always thought we were making a black comedy."

McDowell and Kubrick got on very well when making A Clockwork Orange, despite the vigorous filming regime, yet when the film was done, they never spoke again. In The Complete Kubrick however, it is reported that McDowell and Kubrick went nose to nose after the director left him standing in the shower in preparation for a scene when he needed to be drenched through with rain. McDowell called him "a creep" and apparently there was a face off, after which Malcolm claims the atmosphere was never quite the same again between them. Kubrick severed Malcolm from his life, and over the next couple of decades he spoke rather ill of the director. Now though he remembers him fondly.

"Well, he was very pleasant to be around, to be honest," McDowell told Den Of Geek. "He was a very intelligent man, who knew something about pretty much everything. I used to tease him, because I couldn't get into this whole reverence thing – you know, working with a god or something like that. So I used to pull his leg a lot, and we'd play ping-pong a lot. Ping-pong is one game I'm really good at, and I used to thrash him a lot. But I did decline to play chess with him, because I knew that he was a grand master. He was my director, and that's enough of the power going to him – if I beat him at ping-pong, then I get a little bit of it back."

Unarguably the most iconic of all Kubrick's films, A Clockwork Orange is now a "woop and holler" picture, where screenings are rowdy events of fan fare and celebration. What once shocked and sent viewers into vomiting frenzies, now amuses them. McDowell himself recently attended a screening of the film, after which he was set to take part in a Q and A. Before the event began, McDowell was informed that there was a huge line outside of people dressed as droogs. "Oh," groaned Malcolm, "it's gonna be one of *those* nights..."

BARRY LYNDON (1975)

"For Kubrick, everything has become serious. The way he's been working, in self-willed isolation, with each film consuming years of anxiety, there's no ground between masterpiece and failure. And the pressure shows."

- Pauline Kael on Barry Lyndon

One of the truly great things about Kubrick's small but hugely influential and important filmography is the fact that as you age, the films age with you. Most young people getting into Kubrick, these days at least, will dive straight in for the cult delights of A Clockwork Orange, often relishing the devilish antics and dark humour without taking home the film's true message or meaning. As you get a little older, you'll enjoy the visual mastery of 2001, the humour of Dr. Strangelove and the Freudian discomforts of Lolita. A work like The Shining is so engraved into the public consciousness that most people aren't aware, on entry level into that dark universe, that it's a Kubrick film at all. I know I had no idea as a child who the director was, but the images were so strong and imprinted into every groove in my mind from a very young age that you knew the filmmaker just had to be someone special.

Once you've scratched the Kubrick surface, into the dark real life horror of Full Metal Jacket and the erotic discomforts of Eyes Wide Shut, you're hooked in deep. Barry Lyndon is one of the Kubrick films that a lot of people will find slightly underwhelming at first, an over long treat for the eyes that arguably does little for the soul, brain or the heart. As a visual spectacle, it's undeniably good, but as a film in its own right, it takes some time to appreciate it.

The picture had taken years for Kubrick to prepare and he took extra care in every single second, each tiny frame, to ensure this was his most beautiful, graceful and classy picture yet. But it was a box office failure, while some critics had problems with it, and he was hurt by the more cruel reactions. Though most had to admit it looked good, a number of reviewers noted there was very little under the surface to admire. It was style over content, a snooze fest, and on my own first viewing I couldn't help but agree with them that, indeed, Barry Lyndon was Kubrick's dud. This was the early 2000s and I was enamoured with the recently unleashed A Clockwork Orange as a 15 year old lad, upon Kubrick's death and the lift of its UK ban. This was the ultimate teen flick, a tale of angst, arrogance and anarchy that appealed to my spotty self back when school was offering no solutions. Ten years on and I was slightly less obsessed with Alex's sneering attitude, and was mature enough to find beauty in the more neglected of Kubrick's movies, namely the elegant Barry Lyndon. Though often painfully slow and one note, it's a smooth film that washes over you, and even becomes soothing on repeated viewings, where hidden subtleties and shades come to the fore.

Set in 18th Century Ireland, it follows Ryan O'Neal as Redmond Barry during his various misadventures after fleeing from the police to Dublin, after he believes he has killed an army captain called John Quin. He enlists in the army, and soon discovers that Quin didn't in fact die, and the death was faked so that his cousin Nora's family could get Barry out of the picture in favour of someone with money. Lyndon heads for the Seven Years War in Germany, and then becomes a servant for the Chevalier de Balibari. In Belgium, he marries a widow, the Countess of Lyndon, and takes her name. The film then charts Barry's descent into moral corruption, living off his wife's wealth, bullying his step son, and frolicking with other women while locking his wife away. As things go down hill for him, he turns to alcoholism after the loss of his son.

Barry Lyndon runs at over three hours, but there are enough changes and varying moods in it to keep the attention. With its ramblingly long story, Lyndon is much more a sprawling novel than a paced film in its own right (someone once called it the thinking man's Forest Gump), and taken on its own terms is a very effective piece. O'Neal is suitably caddish as Barry, convincingly taking his character through various personal peaks and troughs with sincerity, and he is clearly relishing the chance to play such a complex and flawed man.

Though O'Neal may be the film's literal star, the real star is of course Stanley Kubrick, who amazes with his sharp focus and ability to present some of the most stunning visuals from the golden age of 1970s cinema. Kubrick excels in slow zooms, beautiful long shots, perfectly framed scenarios and neat composition. The master is at work in full bloom here.

To understand why he made Barry Lyndon, you need to look at Kubrick's place in cinema at that moment in time. After two big hits, 2001 and A Clockwork Orange, Kubrick was a genuine "name" director, the controversial perfectionist who demanded the best from his co workers and delivered the best to his audiences. He was now the private recluse of cinema legend, living quietly in England away from the flashing bulbs of the press, the probing microphones of reporters and the razzle-dazzle red carpet fakery of Hollywood. He was famous, but no one knew what he looked like. As his step daughter Katharina later noted, he had the best of both worlds; acclaim and anonymity.

The big project in the late 1960s after 2001 had been his planned Napoleon epic, but when it fell by the wayside, he felt it was still possible to make a grand film of such a scale, not just a period piece, but *the* period piece of its age. Setting in on William Makepeace Thackeray's novel, The Luck of Barry Lyndon, he had the perfect story to deliver the world an epic costume drama, but importantly a film that was also still very personal. What did Kubrick relate to in his pitiful anti hero? He must have warmed to him somehow, despite his shortcomings as a man. Like Martin Scorsese finally seeing a hint of himself in Jake La Motta, thus prompting him to finally commit to making Raging Bull, Kubrick had to connect with his central characters on a human level, otherwise it couldn't work. For a man so known for combining visuals and music, Kubrick rarely gets the credit he deserves for his characterisations, and his knack of turning people from one dimensional creations on a page to complex multi faceted human beings. With Lyndon, Kubrick gets right under his skin, and though we rarely like the man, we cannot help but guiltily admire his wiliness.

In a fascinating interview with Michael Ciment, he elaborated on his choice to film Barry Lyndon. "I have had a complete set of Thackeray sitting on my bookshelf at home for years, and I had to read several of his novels before reading Barry Lyndon," Kubrick said. "At one time, Vanity Fair interested me as a possible film but, in the end, I decided the story could not be successfully compressed into the relatively short time-span of a feature film. This problem of length, by the way, is now wonderfully accommodated for by the television miniseries which, with its ten to twelve-hour length, pressed on consecutive nights, has created a completely different dramatic form. Anyway, as soon as I read Barry Lyndon I became very excited about it. I loved the story and the characters, and it seemed possible to make the transition from novel to film without destroying it in the process. It also offered the opportunity to do one of the things that movies can do better than any other art form, and that is to present historical subject matter. Description is not one of the things that novels do best but it is something that movies do effortlessly, at least with respect to the effort required of the audience. Barry Lyndon is a story which does not depend upon surprise. What is important is not what is going to happen, but how it will happen. I think Thackeray trades off the advantage of surprise to gain a greater sense of inevitability and a better integration of what might otherwise seem melodramatic or contrived."

Filming began in Spring of 1973 and went on for 300 days, right until early 1974. The production was shrouded in secrecy, as was Kubrick's want, and it was a similarly drawn out process capturing the beauty of the Irish countryside and its expansive mansions. While some critics have seen it as a prime example of how Kubrick really was the actor's director, a master with an ensemble cast of character faces, for me the film is much more of a staged and mannered assemblage of a multitude of elements; furniture, wallpaper and people all being one and the same. The characters are good, but in Barry Lyndon they often seem secondary to the very idea of attempting to make the ultimate period piece. Despite Kubrick making Lyndon an iconic film figure, the locations, equally beautiful and vulgar in their extravagance, are the film's true focus.

Director of Photography John Alcott explained to American Cinematographer how he helped to capture the dazzling visual beauty of Barry Lyndon: "In most instances we were trying to create the feeling of natural light within the houses, mostly stately homes, that we used as shooting locations. That was virtually their only source of light during the period of the film, and those houses still exist, with their paintings and tapestries hanging. I would tend to re-create that type of light, all natural light actually coming through the windows. I've always been a natural light source type of cameraman - if one can put it that way. I think it's exciting, actually, to see what illumination is provided by daylight and then try to create the effect. At the same time, we tried to duplicate the situations established by research and reference to the drawings and paintings of that day - how rooms were illuminated, and so on. The actual compositions of our setups were very authentic to the drawings of the period."

To Kubrick's credit, he succeeded in making a costume drama that didn't look like any of the other costume dramas of the time. The wardrobe department excelled itself, adding realistic grace to the characters, and by not using creaky sets but the real places themselves, he lent the film a genuine authenticity. Without the control and attention to each shot, each location, each costume, each and every line and the manner in which it was delivered, Barry Lyndon could have ended up a hollow, overblown shell. As much as we love reading how eccentric and supposedly frustrating Kubrick's obsessive qualities were, these films would be shadows of themselves without such research and hard work.

You only have to look at interviews Stanley gave at the time to see how much effort went into the movie. "I suppose you could say it is a bit like being a detective," Stanley said of his research for Barry Lyndon. "I accumulated a very large picture file of drawings and paintings taken from art books. These pictures served as the reference for everything we needed to make -- clothes, furniture, hand props, architecture, vehicles, etc. Good research is an absolute necessity and I enjoy doing it. You have an important reason to study a subject in much greater depth than you would ever have done otherwise, and then you have the satisfaction of putting the knowledge to immediate good use. The designs for the clothes were all copied from drawings and paintings of the period. None of them were designed in the normal sense. What is very important is to get some actual clothes of the period to learn how they were originally made. To get them to look right, you really have to make them the same way. Consider also the problem of taste in designing clothes, even for today. Only a handful of designers seem to have a sense of what is striking and beautiful. How can a designer, however brilliant, have a feeling for the clothes of another period which is equal to that of the people and the designers of the period itself, as recorded in their pictures? I spent a year preparing Barry Lyndon before the shooting began and I think this time was very well spent."

Though not the "coolest" or "sexiest" of Kubrick films, it's essential viewing, and only when viewing it four or five times does the film start to become enjoyable. The prospect of Barry Lyndon to someone revved up by the steamy eroticism of Eyes Wide Shut, the violence and snarling humour of A Clockwork Orange, or the demonic horrors of The Shining might be turned off at the prospect of Ryan O'Neal poncing about with Ireland's hoity upper classes for three hours. At first, it can seem too heavy, too dour and a little intimidating, but over time the film shows its low key magic. It's like a three hour painting, Kubrick's tour de force in visuals.

Out of all Kubrick's films, you cannot get past the fact that Barry Lyndon did receive the most underwhelming notices. It is, I have to say, my least favourite of his post Lolita run of films; but in such an illustrious 13 film CV, this doesn't make it bad at all. Some reviewers were slightly disrespectful, and the film underperformed at the box office, but it did have its fans. New York Times liked it, but also found it emotionally uninvolving. They wrote the following: "Barry Lyndon, Stanley Kubrick's handsome, assured screen adaptation of William Makepeace Thackeray's first novel, is so long and leisurely, so panoramic in its narrative scope, that it's as much an environment as it is a conventional film. Mr. Kubrick has spent a fortune on the film, and it shows. One of Mr. Kubrick's boldest decisions was to make the film as beautiful as it is. Good movies should not be too beautiful. It's thought to be distracting, if not a substitute for content. Yet the Alcott camerawork, which transforms scene after scene into something that suggests a Gainsborough or a Watteau, has the function of setting us apart from Barry's adventures, rather than tricking us into involvement."

"Casting, concept and execution are all superb," Variety noted, "Kubrick's outstanding external landscapes – in rich, cool tones – overpower the ant-like people crawling about; his interiors – hot, uncomfortable despite their plushness – seem unnatural in contrast.

This cinematic mural bears repeated and sustained watching without ever really commanding and demanding acute attention. Could anyone else have pulled this off? Not since the days of those great David O. Selznick-George Cukor productions."

Kubrick himself defended his film, and pointed out the ridiculous structure of the movie review business. "To see a film once and write a review is an absurdity," Kubrick said to John Hofsess in a piece entitled How I Learned to Stop Worrying and Love Barry Lyndon. "Yet very few critics ever see a film twice or write about films from a leisurely, thoughtful perspective. The reviews that distinguish most critics, unfortunately, are those slambang pans which are easy to write and fun to write and absolutely useless. There's not much in a critic showing off how clever he is at writing silly, supercilious gags about something he hates."

But one cannot totally argue with some of the reviewer's gripes. Pauline Kael, the legendary film critic herself, admired the film's look but was well observed when she thought it never truly came to life. "As it becomes apparent that we are to sit and admire the lingering tableaux, we feel trapped," Kael spat. "It's not merely that Kubrick isn't releasing the actors' energies or the story's exuberance but that he's deliberately holding the energy level down. He sets up his shots peerlessly, and can't let go of them. There are scenes, such as the card-room argument between Barry and the gouty old Sir Charles Lyndon (Frank Middlemass), that just sit there on the screen, obsessively, embarrassingly. Kubrick has worked them out visually, but dramatically they're hopeless. He has written his own screenplay, and the film lacks the tensions and conflicting temperaments that energized some of his earlier work and gave it jazzy undercurrents."

As Kael points out, validly but also rather unfairly, the acting often seems secondary. "In Kubrick's A Clockwork Orange," she continued, "Malcolm McDowell brought his own vitality and instinct to the bullying hero; here Kubrick manipulates the actors the way he did in 2001. The men are country bumpkins or over bred and ugly (they're treated rather like the writer, Patrick Magee, in Clockwork); the women, long-necked and high-breasted, are lovely, but they're no more than the camera's passing fancies. Kubrick doesn't want characterizations from the actors."

Though it would have been an entirely different film, one can't help but feel that Lyndon would have been much more lively and inclusive had he sped up the dialogue, the shots, the scenes and given his characters a little more life. Imagine less gracious camera work, something more vital and alert, but with the same handsome costumes; or maybe some humour thrown in to make Barry a more human and relatable person. With this, Barry Lyndon could have been truly remarkable. In the wake of the lively and wonderful A Clockwork Orange, Barry Lyndon is at times so dead it's like looking at a freeze frame, but a beautiful freeze frame at least. That said, it is its own entity and you can't really take anything away from it.

Barry Lyndon, beneath the glossiness, is a character study of a foolish man overreaching, always wanting more despite having it all. He's unlikeable, charmless and idiotic, a parable for the greedy upper classes. Unlike Alex from A Clockwork Orange, there is no charisma, and O'Neal is no match for McDowell as a leading man. But O'Neal does a fine job, and it fits perfectly with the mood Kubrick establishes.. View Barry Lyndon then as a lesson in filmmaking, purposely restrained, an exercise in grandiose extravagance as high

106

art. Though not a quotable romp or a teenager's poster favourite, Barry Lyndon is undeniably majestic, and as a calling card for Kubrick's abilities to bring whatever he is focusing on to vivid life, it's up there with the best.

THE SHINING (1980)

*"There's something inherently wrong with the human personality.
There's an evil side to it. One of the things that horror stories can do
is to show us the archetypes of the unconscious; we can see the dark
side without having to confront it directly"*
- Stanley Kubrick

Perhaps Stanley Kubrick's most celebrated and dissected film today is his mysterious, multi layered and utterly addictive adaptation of Stephen King's hit horror novel The Shining. Telling the tale of ex alcoholic struggling writer Jack Torrance, who, with his wife Wendy and son Danny, takes over as winter caretaker at the remote and imposing Overlook Hotel, the film descends into a disturbing whirlwind of unexplained (and indeed unexplainable) paranormal encounters, visions, apparitions, symbolic family dynamics, grizzly murder and frightening insanity. Kubrick tackles the horror genre to the ground, mercilessly reshapes it and leaves it there lying in blood. Dare we step nearer to take a closer look?

After the deflating reactions to Barry Lyndon, people have noted that Stanley maybe felt he was lagging behind. Younger directors were coming in and blowing the socks off movie goers and he hadn't caused a serious dint since 1971's A Clockwork Orange. He hadn't intended to make a horror film, but he found himself drawn to the idea of making a decent addition to that genre, as he had with science fiction for 2001. Kubrick had seen William Friedkin craft the ultimate horror experience with 1973's The Exorcist, and knew that if he were going to contribute to the well worn genre, it had to be something extra special. Even at this stage, 25 years into his professional movie career, he had tackled and made the ultimate examples of several key movie genres; the war movie, the crime flick, the historical epic, the anarchic comedy, the risqué study of male sexuality, the ultimate space experience, the violent sci-fi black comedy and the period costume drama. No genre, theme or era was off limits for Stanley and he repeatedly redefined his chosen field with each project he took on. And of course, "took on" is a vast understatement when we are talking about the artistic input of a filmmaker of Stanley's magnitude and his level of passion for the project. Kubrick spent years on his films - researching, designing, casting, and then of course filming - and The Shining was no exception. In fact it proved to be one of the most detailed and thoroughly executed movies of his career.

When I asked Anthony Frewin (Kubrick's long time assistant and now representative of his estate) whether Kubrick had ever really wanted to make a horror film before this, or whether every kind of story was an open ended possibility, he replied with what I really already knew. "I don't think Stanley Kubrick necessarily wanted to make a 'horror' film, if, indeed, that is what The Shining is. What appealed to Stanley was story."

Horror or not, what makes The Shining one of the most important films categorised in the horror genre ever made, and possibly the single most seminal masterpiece of its genre? Well, it's largely because Kubrick manages to "de-schlock" the well worn format and make it an admirable artistic art form, an entity in its own parallel reality which fuses dimensions together, never explains itself and remains a cloaked enigma to the viewer. It is the one Kubrick movie with which you could also be describing the man himself. With his take on The Shining, he gave horror a sense of dignity, style and class. It was a film for the mind, not just a piece of run of the mill gory trash. If Nightmare on Elm Street, for all its minor fun, was a cartoon scribble, then The Shining was the work of Michelangelo. Its iconic stature is also down to the sheer entertainment value, the acting, the dialogue, the memorable images, the disturbing multi layers, the aggressive deconstruction of the American family and so much more besides. There have been books written about Kubrick's take on The Shining, but in this short article I hope to pin point a few factors which have made The Shining a total and utter phenomenon.

It's well documented that Stanley often took years to find the "right" story for his next picture, and it was a highly complex and strange process in itself. He actually had "readers", people employed through his assistant Anthony Frewin who would trawl through books for "Frewin's boss", Kubrick, whose true identity was never revealed to them as they worked their way through stacks of dog eared paperbacks and manuscripts. It was once reported that a stack of horror books made their way right to Kubrick, who could be heard slamming each one against the wall in frustration; until, of course, he got to Stephen King's The Shining. A shame, then, that this story isn't true, even if it is one that many would *like* to be true, adding to the Kubrick mystique.

Kubrick was asked by trusted interviewer Michel Ciment what drew him to the book. He went into a lengthy answer about the film's supernatural elements and how they don't tie the viewer to believing in the ludicrous. "I've always been interested in ESP and the paranormal. In addition to the scientific experiments which have been conducted suggesting that we are just short of conclusive proof of its existence, I'm sure we've all had the experience of opening a book at the exact page we're looking for, or thinking of a friend a moment before they ring on the telephone. But The Shining didn't originate from any particular desire to do a film about this. The manuscript of the novel was sent to me by John Calley, of Warner Bros. I thought it was one of the most ingenious and exciting stories of the genre I had read. It seemed to strike an extraordinary balance between the psychological and the supernatural in such a way as to lead you to think that the supernatural would eventually be explained by the psychological: "Jack must be imagining these things because he's crazy". This allowed you to suspend your doubt of the supernatural until you were so thoroughly into the story that you could accept it almost without noticing. It's what I found so particularly clever about the way the novel was written. As the supernatural events occurred you searched for an explanation, and the most likely one seemed to be that the strange things that were happening would finally be explained as the products of Jack's imagination. It's not until Grady, the ghost of the former caretaker who axed to death his family, slides open the bolt of the larder door, allowing Jack to escape, that you are left with no other explanation but the supernatural. The novel is by no means a serious literary work, but the plot is for the most part extremely well worked out, and for a film that is often all that really matters."

Sets were built at EMI's Elstree Studios in Borehamwood, while the exterior for the hotel itself was the largest ever seen there. To get the interior look just right, Kubrick sent people out all over the world to photograph rooms in countless hotels, and when gathering the photos together, Kubrick selected the décor and furnishings to fit each room in the Overlook exactly. It sounds obsessive, but again, it's the only reason the film looks so perfect.

To give the film a ghostly, spectral quality, and to achieve a singularity in regards to his other films, Stanley enlisted the assistance of Steadicam inventor and technological pioneer Garrett Brown. It was his input in fact which helped make The Shining the very haunting, individual experience it is. The floating cameras helped show the sheer scale of the Overlook, and the tracking shots of the boy created the feeling of a ghostly being endlessly following the occupants around the vast halls and winding corridors. But the modest Brown was not one to boast, and began a fascinating piece he wrote on the making of The Shining for American Cinematographer with a bit of self depreciation:

"To date it cannot be said with complete conviction that the Steadicam has revolutionized the way films are shot," he wrote. "However, it certainly had a considerable effect on the way The Shining was shot. Many of Kubrick's tremendously convoluted sets were designed with the Steadicam's possibilities in mind and were not, therefore, necessarily provided with either flyaway walls or dolly-smooth floors. One set in particular, the giant Hedge Maze, could not have been photographed as Kubrick intended by any other means. I worked on The Shining in England at the EMI Studios in Borehamwood for the better part of a year. I had daily opportunities to test the Steadicam and my operating against the most meticulous possible requirements as to framing accuracy, the ability to hit marks and precision repeatability. I began the picture with years of

112

Steadicam use behind me and with the assumption that I could do with it whatever anyone could reasonably demand. I realized by the afternoon of the first day's work that here was a whole new ball game, and that the word "reasonable" was not in Kubrick's lexicon."

With sets built, Kubrick now needed to cast his picture. The search for Danny, the little boy of the family, took an age and thousands of boys were seen. In the end, the role went to the brilliant Danny Lloyd, who to everyone's loss didn't carry on acting in motion pictures (he's now a teacher). For Wendy, Kubrick cast Shelley Duvall, with whom he would have more than a little friction with during filming. In truth, he pushed her to breaking point to get the right emotions from her performance. As a result, she suffered a bout of ill health. Whether Kubrick was genuinely irritated by her or was pushing right to the limit in order to get the desired fatigued and worn out effect remains a mystery, but as Duvall says in the Making of The Shining, shot by Stanley's daughter Vivian, it was well worth the upset for the finished result. How Duvall feels now is anyone's guess. She was last seen on Dr Phil's TV show and was clearly suffering from a severe mental illness.

The most vital casting was that of the part of Jack Torrance. Never one for huge star names, Kubrick knew it had to be someone with serious ability and charisma, and if they needed to be well known, they had to have the talent to back it up. Years earlier, after seeing him in Easy Rider, Stanley had contacted Jack for the possibility of playing Napoleon in his ill fated attempt at filming the dictator's life story. Jack did a reading for him, but as the project never came to light, that was the end of that. Stanley though, greatly admired Jack and had kept him in mind for future consideration. When it came to The Shining, he had no one else in mind but him.

"I believe that Jack is one of the best actors in Hollywood, perhaps on a par with the greatest stars of the past like Spencer Tracy and Jimmy Cagney," Kubrick said, after adding that Jack was his first choice for the part of Torrance. "I should think that he is on almost everyone's first-choice list for any role which suits him. His work is always interesting, clearly conceived and has the X-factor, magic. Jack is particularly suited for roles which require intelligence. He is an intelligent and literate man, and these are qualities almost impossible to act. In The Shining, you believe he's a writer, failed or otherwise."

The screenplay was knocked out by Kubrick and Diane Johnson, a novelist of whom Kubrick was something of a fan. It proved to be a great pairing and they got along fine as friends and collaborators. "Diane and I talked a lot about the book and then we made an outline of the scenes we thought should be included in the film," Stanley said, revealing what sounds like a fairly straight forward writing process. "This list of scenes was shuffled and reshuffled until we thought it was right, and then we began to write. We did several drafts of the screenplay, which was subsequently revised at different stages before and during shooting."

It soon became apparent that Kubrick wasn't going to follow the book page by page, and he got rid of a few things for starters, like the moving animal hedges, and added in the maze and various other scenes. The ending of the book has the Overlook explode, while Kubrick chose to have Jack freeze to death in the maze while his family escape. Understandably, King himself has since vocalised his distaste for Kubrick's adaptation. In a recent interview he complained, "The character of Jack Torrance has no arc in that movie. Absolutely no arc at all. When we first see Jack Nicholson, he's in the office of Mr. Ullman, the manager of the hotel, and you know, then, he's crazy as a shit house rat. All he does is get crazier. In the book, he's a guy who's struggling with his sanity and finally loses it. To me, that's a tragedy. In the movie, there's no tragedy because there's no real change."

He also thought the film was empty and cold, which he said was his greatest regret, as he feels his books are warm and very inclusive with the reader. But he found The Shining on screen to be depressing, with no resolve or true meaning. "I think The Shining is a beautiful film and it looks terrific and as I've said before, it's like a big, beautiful Cadillac with no engine inside it," he later remarked. "In that sense, when it opened, a lot of the reviews weren't very favourable and I was one of those reviewers. I kept my mouth shut at the time, but I didn't care for it much,"

One of King's major concerns was how Kubrick changed Wendy's character. In the book she is strong, much stronger than Jack Torrance in fact, while in the movie, Shelley Duvall portrays her, perhaps against her own will, as a quivering wreck, put down by her abusive husband who she clearly loves more than he loves her. I believe that because Wendy begins the film so weak and slightly pathetic in the face of Jack's bullying temperament, it makes her resistance in the closing chapters, and her subsequent survival, all the more powerful. But then I didn't write the book. I love King's book, and find it thrilling in its own way, but Kubrick didn't so much adapt it to the screen, but re-imagined, reinterpreted and reinvented

115

it. In the book, the hotel holds the true evil, it's haunted beyond comprehension and Jack, the weak ex drunk failing to stay clean and stable, is dragged down by the horrors of the Overlook. In the film, it's clear that Jack doesn't have all that far to go before hand anyway, and the darkness of the building itself merely absorbs his malevolent evil. Two very different tales, with drastically different messages behind them. Like A Clockwork Orange, it's the contrast between personal choice and inevitability.

I must have seen The Shining over a hundred times now, although I have no real way of knowing the exact figure. Yes, that sounds unhealthy and slightly obsessive (in truth it makes me sound like one of the voices on the charming Shining documentary 237), but this is from the age of 14 or so and in varied forms of viewing. I went through a phase of watching it every week, or at least having it on in the background, and found myself strangely eased and comforted by its atmosphere. Like David Lynch's Eraserhead (a film Stanley screened to the crew during production to signify the vibe he was looking for), it has a menacing air that is also soothing, consistent and smooth. Though disturbing and scary, The Shining is also a film you can enjoy as pure entertainment alone; its iconic scenes, quotable dialogue and powerful imagery make it one of the most enjoyable films of the past fifty years. Though a horror film, it need not be defined as such. It is, essentially, a warning about the dangers of the human mind, with very dark humour, charismatic performances and some of the most unforgettable moments in movie history to boot.

The film has so many layers to it that there have been vast volumes dedicated to it, namely the essential and now very collectable Studies in Horror: Stanley Kubrick's The Shining, which features interviews with just about everyone involved in the film and a host of essays dissecting every facet, theme and underlying subtext in the film. Indeed, The Shining seems to have sparked off a whole obsessive sub culture of its own, with tribute websites, theories and documentaries dedicated to its supposed hidden messages and meanings. The plain bonkers but also very watchable documentary Room 237 takes a look at these secret messages and each theory is narrated by a different fan/interpreter of the film. Is it about the Holocaust? Is it about the plight of the American Indians? Are there subtle confessions from Kubrick that he did indeed fake the Apollo 11 moon landings? Can you see his face in the clouds at the start of the film? According to Room 237, the answer to all these questions, and more, is a resounding yes. The truth is, of course, that none of this stuff is true, but it certainly is very entertaining to listen to. The bottom line is that all this obsession is actually harmless. It enhances the myth of an already mythical film and makes Stanley Kubrick even more of a legendary figure. It's also a fitting tribute to the power of The Shining, a film crammed full of wacky ideas, morbid complexities, heavyweight metaphors, and frightening mystery.

It's amazing to think that The Shining, a film now so cemented into film legend, actually received a mixed reception at the time of its release. As is the case with all of Kubrick's work though, first and second viewings are but a drop in the ocean in fully understanding the film in question. Over time, The Shining would gain popularity, slowly climbing the ranks as his most adored and well known picture.

In their review at the time, New York Times were one of the underwhelmed voices, who praised Jack's "devilishly funny" performance, but seemed uncommitted to anything else. The segment reading, "The Shining begins to show traces of sensationalism, and the effects don't necessarily pay off. The film's climactic chase virtually fizzles out before it reaches a resolution," best illustrates their lack of excitement for the movie.

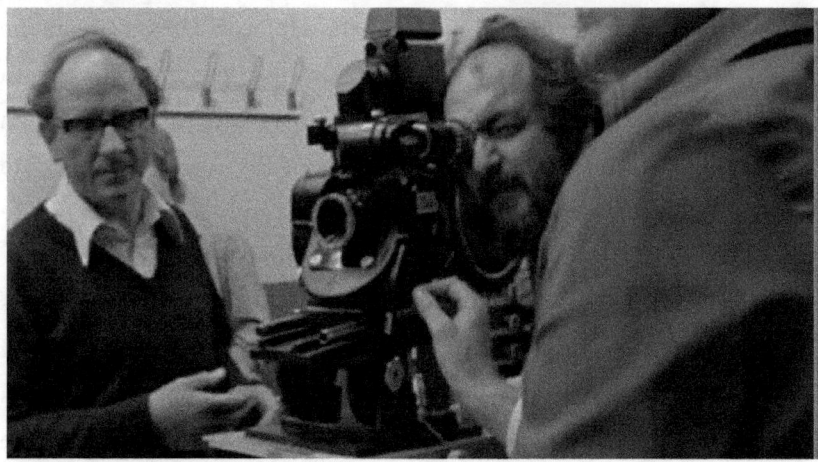

Variety seemed to hate everything about the film, savagely writing, "With everything to work with, director Stanley Kubrick has teamed with jumpy Jack Nicholson to destroy all that was so terrifying about Stephen King's bestseller. In his book, King took a fundamental horror formula – an innocent family marooned in an evil dwelling with a grim history – and built layers of ingenious terror upon it. The father is gradually possessed by the demonic, desolate hotel. With dad going mad, the only protection mother and child have is the boy's clairvoyance – his 'shining' – which allows him an innocent understanding and some ability to outmanoeuvre the devils. But Kubrick sees things his own way, throwing 90% of King's creation out.

118

The crazier Nicholson gets, the more idiotic he looks. Shelley Duvall transforms the warm sympathetic wife of the book into a simpering, semi-retarded hysteric."

By the decade's end however there was something of a turnaround in the film's appreciation, which seems to be rocketing more and more with each passing year. It's now taken on a life of its own, and like A Clockwork Orange, has become a mythical piece separate from the rest of Kubrick's illustrious filmography.

The appeal lies in the mystery, the fact that so little is truly explained and defined. Modern film is all too blatant, and the intentions and meanings are as clear as day, revealed to us by the filmmakers during the duration of the picture. Kubrick - in all his films but especially with The Shining - invited us to make up our own minds, come forth with theories and ideas. He also encouraged repeated viewings, where each sitting revealed a new layer, a new level of potentially decipherable puzzles. There's a dark, unexplained void in the centre of The Shining and it's there for us all to fill in our own way. Are there ghosts in the Overlook, or is everything stirred and brewed up by the power of the human mind, the darkest machine of all? A firm belief in the afterlife is not essential in taking away satisfaction from The Shining, and unlike modern schlock horror films like Paranormal Activity and such, the viewer is not told what to see, believe and feel. The surrealist in all of us can delight in the visions throughout The Shining, and the philosopher in us can ponder, theorise and dissect until the cows come home. For a director to leave their film so open is rare these days, but with The Shining, Kubrick invited us all along for the ride, despite what King might have said about its apparent coldness.

FULL METAL JACKET (1987)

'I once described 1980-83 as a single phone call lasting three years, with interruptions. I'd think, doesn't this guy get tired?"
- Collaborator Michael Herr

A few years ago I spoke with horror special effects legend and Vietnam veteran Tom Savini about the films that best captured the nightmare of that particular war. "Platoon came pretty close and not surprising as Oliver Stone is a Vietnam vet," Savini explained to me, "but also surprising to me that he didn't put in little details that no one knows about unless they've been there, like how we moved Vietcong bodies out of the way with como wire, waiting till rigor set in to put one wire behind the head and another around the feet to lift and toss them into trucks. The Deer Hunter had some very real emotional editing in it, when one minute they are having fun in the states, and the very next minute they are there in the Jungle. This is how it felt. You didn't believe you were there, and that jump in time was real and felt real to me when I saw it." Savini ended his explanation with this: "Full Metal Jacket was the best as far as the feeling of really being there..." It figures.

By the time Kubrick started making Full Metal Jacket, the Vietnam war was long over, though its after effects were still very much being felt across America. Veterans were the country's forgotten men, unwanted, spat at, and called baby killers. Many were descending into depressive lives of drug addiction and eventually suicide. Vietnam had been a major embarrassment for America, an ugly part of its history, and the whole mess was being swept under the carpet. Out of sight, out of mind was the general feeling. However, the years following the end of the war had seen a steady flow of pictures highlighting the sheer horror of that most pointless of wars. Films like Coming Home and The Deer Hunter had been the Oscar sweepers, the high profile anti-'Nam flicks that did good box office while also hammering their message home. The most bombastic and chaotic 'Nam movie was undoubtedly Francis Ford Coppola's Apocalypse Now, a film that totally captured the madness of the war. As Coppola himself said, "my film is not about Vietnam, it IS Vietnam," and you can't really disagree with that statement.

One of the more low key 'Nam films came in 1977 with Tracks, directed by Henry Jaglom and starring Dennis Hopper as a mentally shredded vet escorting his dead friend across the country on a very long train ride. It was a film that captured the after effects of conflict brilliantly, and unflinchingly, with Hopper's character spiralling into madness as the picture reaches its dazzling climax. But the 'Nam films kept coming. The year before Full Metal Jacket finally saw release, Oliver Stone's shocking and brilliant Platoon emerged, and afterwards, stand outs like De Palma's Casualties of War and the De Niro vehicle Jacknife showed us other viewpoints of the war's impact on certain individuals. Full Metal Jacket exists in its own little pocket of the Vietnam movie genre, just as one would expect from a Stanley Kubrick picture. It's the one that captures best how a group of normal young men can be transformed into emotionless killers.

The genesis of the movie went right back to the early 80s, after Kubrick had finished The Shining, when he contacted the author of the Vietnam memoir Dispatches, by Michael Herr. The initial idea was for them to collaborate on a Holocaust film, but by 1982 this had changed to adapting Gustav Hasford's book The Short Timers, which Kubrick loved. And so, Herr and Kubrick agreed to take on the script together.

Writing later of his experiences with Stanley, Vietnam veteran Herr offered some interesting view points on the director. "I don't want to give the impression that I didn't get extremely irritated, that I never thought he was a cheap prick, that his demands and requirements weren't just TOO MUCH. They say Kubrick had no personal life, that's ridiculous. It would be more correct to say that he had no professional life, since everything he did was personally done. He didn't want to make an anti-war film, he just wanted to depict war. He wanted to show what war is like."

"The whole area of combat was one complete area," Kubrick said to Rolling Stone in 1987. "It actually exists. One of the things I tried to do was give you a sense of where you were, where everything else was. Which, in war movies, is something you frequently don't get. The terrain of small-unit action is really the story of the action. And this is something we tried to make beautifully clear: there's a low wall, there's the building space. And once you get in there, everything is exactly where it actually was. No cutting away, no cheating."

Authenticity is what he was after. After all, this was the man who had once said "real is good but interesting is better," and Full Metal Jacket would become his most "real" picture of all. Shaky, unstable, traumatic and raw, it's his least polished and most harrowing film. The Shining disturbed with its surreal horror, but Full Metal Jacket disturbed with the real life horrors of combat, by showing what men were willing to do to one another when told loud enough.

Tackling Gustav's book was a feat Kubrick wanted to pull off, and he desperately wanted to meet the author himself, a damaged Vietnam vet who Herr knew would be difficult. "I advised him against it," Herr told the Guardian. "I told Stanley I didn't think they'd get on." When Gustav was called over to meet with Stanley for a meeting about the adaptation, Herr's suspicions proved correct, when Kubrick handed him a note which read 'I can't deal with this man.' Gustav was no longer needed from then on.

"I was there for a while and I was just doing all the tourist things," Gustav later said, "and Michael Herr and I went out to Stanley's house and met him. I mean, we'd talked on the phone before, and when I got to England, we were still talking on the phone. Now pretty much every day we were talking on the phone about the film and it was getting more and more detailed all the time." Though shoved out of the way for the adaptation process, Gustav wanted a full screen credit, not just the dialogue credit Stanley had in mind for him. "For a year and a half we were in disagreement," he complained. "From my point of view, I deserved a full credit. I heard all the arguments against my attitude from Stanley and Warner Bros. and Michael Herr, and I was never convinced their arguments were valid. I persisted until I'd won."

Before shooting began, Kubrick spent a long time researching the war, watching footage, documentaries and reading endlessly through the archives. Again, the painstaking research seemed eccentric and obsessive, but if Stanley really wanted to make an authentic war picture, where you could literally *feel* the earth shaking with the heavy explosives and hear the bullets whizzing past your ear, then such research was essential.

Filming commenced in Cambridgeshire, remarkably, given the genuine 'Nam-ish quality of the surroundings when seen up on the big screen. He constructed sets at Millennium Mills, the gas works in Beckton, and even in East London. A non-flyer reluctant to leave the UK, Kubrick brought Vietnam to England, and somehow pulled it all off. Kubrick found the experience of bringing the book to life with the talented young cast an enjoyable experience, and behind the scenes footage shows him in charge but light in mood, even laughing with the actors. He is also clearly frustrated at times, hoping to get the feel just right. But his hard work paid off. The shaky camera work gets you right in the middle of the grizzly action, and the cast are a fantastic ensemble. Kubrick proved that he was the true master of bringing novels to the screen, and he seemed able to excel in any genre he approached. Consider the differences between the sci-fi comedy-drama A Clockwork Orange, the surreal horrors of The Shining and the gritty war study Full Metal Jacket, and you realise what a remarkable range Stanley really had.

To Rolling Stone, Kubrick spoke of the process of shifting published words from another writer's mind to movies of his own imagination. "What I like about not writing original material - which I'm not even certain I could do - is that you have this tremendous advantage of reading something for the first time. You never have this experience again with the story. You have a reaction to it: it's a kind of falling-in-love reaction. That's the first thing. Then it becomes almost a matter of code breaking, of breaking the work down into a structure that is truthful, that doesn't lose the ideas or the content or the feeling of the book. And fitting it all into the much more limited time frame of a movie. And as long as you possibly can, you retain your emotional attitude, whatever it was that made you fall in love in the first place. You judge a scene by asking yourself, Am I still responding to what's there? The process is both analytical and emotional. You're trying to balance calculating analysis against feeling. And it's almost never a question of What does this scene mean? It's Is this truthful, or does something about it feel false? It's Is this scene interesting? Will it make me feel the way I felt when I first fell in love with the material? It's an intuitive process, the way I imagine writing music is intuitive. It's not a matter of structuring an argument."

Technically, Stanley made another masterpiece, no question, with a film that tells us that war is VERY bad in the most simple terms, but never preaches; nor does it become overly sentimental, emotionally manipulative or schmaltzy, which is the key in honestly presenting the viewer with such a moralistic dilemma as war. People accuse Kubrick of being a cold filmmaker, but it just isn't true. The only difference is that Kubrick uses emotions differently, not opting for the kind of obviousness favoured in mainstream Hollywood, but for a more stylised, conceptual overall feel in which emotions, feelings and humanity are equal ingredients. We feel for the men in Full Metal Jacket, but they never become pitiful figures, walking political statements for Kubrick to blatantly use as symbols of a corrupt country and its dishonest, improper world pursuits. Nothing is quite so bare and naked in a Kubrick film. We make up our own minds, and there are enough gaps there for us to fill in with our own meanings. Full Metal Jacket is no exception.

While the major drug issue of Vietnam is ignored, the macho posturing and manly camaraderie is captured better than it is in any other 'Nam film. Though some critics called it an empty vessel that has no real inner core, the lack of a central message is also its biggest statement. After all, to these young guys, drafted and dragged away from their homes to fight a pointless war, this whole excursion had no inner core. The whole thing was a mess which made little sense, and by depicting the young cast as hopeless and helpless pawns in a bloody game of chess, Kubrick has captured the meaninglessness of battle more than any other director ever did.

From the angry drill sergeant played by R. Lee Ermey to the wide eyed performance from Matthew Modine as Joke Davis, every section of the cast is excellent. Even though the technicalities are perfect, without the convincing performances the film would have fallen face flat. Kubrick, ever a master of casting, managed to find the perfect man for each role. The real movie stealer though has to be Vincent D'Onofrio, who gives one of the strongest and most unsettling performances from all of Kubrick's films. Gaining 70 pounds for the role of the troubled Leonard Lawrence, who eventually snaps and has one of the most memorable and horrific scenes in film history, he is an utter revelation.

"Yeah, it was my first feature," Vincent told Star Pulse in 2009. "Basically all I can really remember is not wanting to get fired. Because there were people being fired and so I just wanted to do it right. I was still studying method acting at the time, so I was in touch with my teacher about it when I was in England. I would talk to her occasionally about what I was doing and she would just confirm things - that I was on the right track and stuff. It was basically for me just about hanging in there and not getting fired by one of the best directors that we've ever had or will ever have, one of the best. It was scary because of that and I hoped that if I just stuck with what I thought I knew best I would be okay... and it turned out alright. "

Vincent has the honour of being the focal point of one of Stanley's most iconic scenes. His sinister, demented face, after slaughtering the drill sergeant and before pulling the gun on himself, is up there with the image of an eye lash wearing Malcolm McDowell in A Clockwork Orange. Both penetrate the camera and are very iconic, powerful images that refuse to leave the mind. Again, nearly 40 years into his filmmaking career, Kubrick could pull absolutely stunning images out of nowhere which burned immediately into your brain, remaining there forever.

Structurally, Full Metal Jacket captures the constant looming threat of a war, and by dividing itself into two parts - the training and the combat - it juxtaposes the harsh difference between before and during the fight, capturing the state of shock one must undoubtedly feel when going in. The harassing boot camp segment reminds one of the invasive prison scenes in A Clockwork Orange, with Kubrick taking note once again of the state's control over the individual. They are shaved, stripped of their own identity and rebranded.

The critics at the time though - again, as with most Kubrick movies - were not impressed, and saw the film as derivative of earlier war flicks, and mostly aimless in its depictions of human suffering and the brutality of battle. Like Jack Torrance in The Shining, and Alex in A Clockwork Orange, the young soldiers in Full Metal Jacket are the little men out of their depth, unable to control the situations they are in. In The Shining it's the supernatural powers, in A Clockwork Orange it's the government, and in Full Metal Jacket it's the military. We're all in a prison of some sort. But the naysayers couldn't grasp such a simple concept. Seven years on from his last movie The Shining, the feedback given to Full Metal Jacket at the time was underwhelming to say the least. This was not, many agreed, a grand artistic statement, nor did it have very much of its own to say about war. Was this really the man who gave us 2001: A Space Odyssey?

"It's one of the best-looking war movies ever made on sets and stages," Roger Ebert said of the picture in his mixed review, adding, "but that's not good enough when compared to the awesome reality of Platoon, Apocalypse Now and The Deer Hunter. The crucial last passages of the film too often look and feel like World War II films from Hollywood studios. We see the same sets from so many different angles that after the movie we could find our own way around Kubrick's Vietnam. Time and again in the film, we get great shots with no payoffs. Full Metal Jacket is uncertain where to go, and the movie's climax, which Kubrick obviously intends to be a mighty moral revelation, seems phoned in from earlier war pictures. After what has already been said about Vietnam in the movies, Full Metal Jacket is too little and too late."

New York Times were slightly more impressed, writing, "Full Metal Jacket, Mr. Kubrick's harrowing, beautiful and characteristically eccentric new film about Vietnam, is going to puzzle, anger and (I hope) fascinate audiences as much as any film he has made to date. The movie, opening today at the National and other theatres, will inevitably be compared with Oliver Stone's Platoon, but its narrative is far less neat and cohesive - and far more antagonistic - than Mr. Stone's film."

The Washington Post were one of the loudest fans of the film, writing, "There's a major star in Full Metal Jacket: Stanley Kubrick's direction. Resurfacing like a cinematic cicada after a seven-year absence, the American expatriate has overtaken the home grown Viet Pack of Coppolas, Ciminos and Stones to make the most eloquent and exacting vision of the war to date. Inspired with technique rather than overblown with it, Kubrick, the filmmaker's filmmaker, lays one on you."

Full Metal Jacket is possibly Kubrick's most direct and conventional movie, even if it does have its own share of surrealistic ghostliness too. The finale with the sniper is one of the most tense and exciting sequences in war movie history, and Kubrick handles the tension with masterful ease. This is a powerful film in all regions, from the spellbinding performances and the breathtaking sights, to the highly quotable dialogue that lifts it into being Kubrick's most human piece of filmmaking, alongside perhaps Eyes Wide Shut. Thirty years on, it's aging very well, whereas other 'Nam films are not fairing too well. Kubrick may have come relatively late to this particular subject, but it can be argued that he was the only one, Coppola aside, to really put his own stamp on it one hundred percent and transcend the sub-genre. This is a Kubrick film through and through, from the tiniest detail to the most glaringly obvious.

EYES WIDE SHUT (1999)

"Nicole and I talk about it so much at night. When we're 70 years old, sitting on the front porch, we'll be able to look back and say, 'Wow! We made this movie with Stanley Kubrick!' We know it may take a long time to finish, but we don't care. We really don't."

- Tom Cruise, 1996

By the 1990s, Stanley Kubrick was seen as a legendary recluse, rumours about whom bordered on the highly sensational. He was, according to press reports, a mad man, a hermit, a megalomaniac and general odd ball. His films, as eccentric and wild as he, were windows, portals you might say, into his dark and mysterious soul. Stanley, an archivist who kept every cutting and article about himself, must surely have been amused by such nonsense.

In reality, Stanley was a work from home dad who cared for his kids, looked after his cats and took on film projects from the comfort of his own abode. "He didn't *need* to leave," Leon Vitali, his assistant and friend said in one documentary on Stanley. When he did go out, he'd nip to Ryman's stationery store in St. Albans to check out the binders, note pads and accessories. He always paid in cash, so the cashier wouldn't see the name and link him to those mythical films of his. Being recognised would have been too embarrassing for him.

Behind closed doors and away from the myth of being the mad genius the world saw him to be, he was busy working on film projects. After Full Metal Jacket, he had explored possible new ideas, one being a film about the Holocaust. He became obsessed with the subject, but after Steven Spielberg emerged with his masterpiece Schindler's List, he abandoned the project. (There is a chapter at the end of the book which goes into more detail about Kubrick's unfinished movie projects.)

The real germs of his next movie, Eyes Wide Shut, first surfaced in the early 1960s, when Stanley had the idea to make a film about a couple and their sexual relations. As the decades went on, names were attached (Steve Martin and Woody Allen to name two), and varied approaches were pondered, but nothing in that area really came to light. Kubrick had read the 1926 book Dream Story, written by Arthur Schitzler, and was inspired by the tale. Shaking it up and bringing it into modern day, he invited screenwriter Frederic Raphael to collaborate on a screenplay. For Kubrick, this was an interesting story with a lot of cinematic potential. Though updated and altered from the book, and more openly erotic in its mood, Stanley had found the perfect story after years of searching.

Warner Brothers had suggested Kubrick cast a star in his next picture to play the husband, and he opted for Tom Cruise. Cruise went over to meet Stanley in a helicopter, and later Kubrick asked Kidman if she would play the wife. "I'd have said yes if I'd have had one line," she confessed. They were to play William and Alice Harford, a doctor and art curator respectively, who begin to see through the surface of their marriage. After a high society function, where they both flirt hopelessly with other people, they return home to their apartment, a little inebriated to say the least, and Alice confesses dark lustful fantasies while high on pot. Her lurid tale disturbs him, and he begins to wonder if he really truly knows his wife, the mother of his child. Suspicious and curious, a whole world of jealousy opens up, and Bill finds himself pulled into a strange web of murkiness, a night long odyssey of self discovery, introspection, masked orgies, mysterious deaths and seedy shenanigans aplenty.

Filming started in November of 1996, after years of preparation, including the sending out of scouts to photograph locations in order to get the look just right. Exact street widths of Manhattan stretches were even taken down, in order to replicate, perfectly no less, those New York streets at Pinewood Studios. Again, there was no possibility of Kubrick leaving England to film, even for two major stars like Cruise and Kidman... they had to come to him, and that was that!

Eyes Wide Shut is one of Kubrick's most beautiful looking films, and each prop, costume, movement and shot seems to have been considered to the smallest detail. All these details though, however minute and seemingly inconsequential, add up to the complete final picture. The streets, recreated precisely to his liking, feel more like New York in a dream, and there is an added ghostliness to the corners, doorways and roads that puts the film up there with The Shining as a surrealist horror painting. This time however, the horror is not of the axe wielding father possessed by evil spirits variety, but a fear on the hidden, possibly totally imagined secrets of a marriage, and in the underbelly of high class city life. Cruise's character knows there are shady and sleazy things going on out there in the world, and when he has brushes with them, he is disturbed. Lured to the dark side, after realising he was way more hurt than he thought he would be at the thought of his wife having sexual fantasies about other men, he dips his toe into the murkiness under the surface, but realises that world isn't for him. It's a scary place, and he's out of his depth. Cruise knows where he belongs, back with his family in that cosy, warmly lit apartment; eyes closed to the hidden desires and deadly temptations of the world. He was a little too smug before, complacent and taking his wife for granted. And if he has learned anything in the end of his adventure, then it's not to take anything for granted, especially life itself.

When all the mysteries of the plot are laid to rest, Sydney Pollack as Victor Zeigler wraps up the picture with the blunt statement, "Nobody killed anybody. Someone died - it happens all the time. Life goes on, until it doesn't." And for Stanley, not long after filming finished, life no longer went on. He had prepared a cut and showed it to his two stars. Under a week after the screening, Stanley was dead.

Of course, there were other after effects of the film too, namely the divorce of Cruise and Kidman. Some claimed their relationship was struggling before this and that the tension and strain of filming Eyes Wide Shut put the final nail in the coffin. Nicole Kidman herself recently spoke about working with Stanley, and also went into the supposed tensions between her and Cruise on set:

"People thought that making the film was the beginning of the end of my marriage, but I don't really think it was. Tom and I were close then. Stanley wanted to use our marriage as a supposed reality. That was Stanley. He used the movie as provocation, pretending it was our sex life -- which we weren't oblivious to, but obviously it wasn't us. We both decided to dedicate ourselves to a great filmmaker and artist. Stanley had to coax me into some of the sexuality in the film in the beginning, but we shot things that were a lot more extreme that didn't end up in the movie. I did feel safe - I never felt it was exploitive or unintelligent."

Forever to be his final curtain, his last cinematic statement to the world of filmgoers who lapped up every frame he had to offer, Eyes Wide Shut is sublime. It's close to being utterly perfect, as you might expect from Kubrick, and it has many layers. There is a discomfort to the film which makes you fidget ever so slightly and consider things from a different angle, especially relationships. Does it matter if ones' partner has sexual fantasies about other people? And what is the difference between imagining one and actually taking part in one? Is Cruise's character a hypocrite for being disturbed by her dreams, considering he was so very close to considering having sex with the two girls at the party? Is his jealousy a typical example of the male ego, the "one rule for her and one rule for him" school of thinking. If he's misogynistic, then his narrow views are challenged during the course of his dark, long and very eventful night on the town.

Kubrick is as masterful as ever throughout the duration of Eyes Wide Shut, his composition, lingering and ghostly camera work lifting the picture from what could have been predictable "erotic thriller" fare. Every shot is a work of art in itself, every gesture from each actor's tiniest moment expertly put across; and like The Shining, not everything is as it seems. Nor is everything explained. The fact he died after its completion and never really got to explain it to us makes the film all the more of an enigma.

Understated and played out with constraint, it's a film with a gorgeously smooth flow to it, and it carries you along its gentle stream, though you hit the odd rock now and then. The tones, all moody blues and reds, give the film its own sense of identity. Again, Kubrick didn't just make another film that fit into a genre already established, he created a new genre. Erotic thriller? Erotic drama?

Neither. Was it, as so many dissectors believe it to be, an uncovering of the hidden fact that a very small number of people are controlling everything in this society which has been constructed just to keep us quiet and in our place? It's hard to say, and that's what makes this one, and the rest of Kubrick's films for that matter, so hard to pigeonhole... but Eyes Wide Shut more so.

"Stanley Kubrick's extraordinary last testament, Eyes Wide Shut, has effortlessly attained one of the criteria of a certain type of classic," the Guardian wrote at the time, in a mixed review that seems a little uneven in retrospect. "It is sui generis in modern Anglophone cinema: in a genre, if not a league, of its own, this genre being best described as Manhattan porn gothic. It has left the global critical community (which has been allowed to view it much earlier and on more generous terms than if the master were still alive) uneasily aware of the possibility that it is not a masterpiece, but rather a grotesque, preposterous flop that embarrassingly damages one of the most unimpeachable reputations in world cinema. Kubrick's last film works only if its satirical, mischievous quality is fully appreciated; as an essay on the nature of sexuality it is vulgar and pretentious, but taken as a bizarre, hallucinatory black comic fable about married life, it is plausible and enjoyable, particularly given the terrific performance by Sydney Pollack as a worldly, libertine party host. The technical and visual command of this movie is captivating - but it is a minor Kubrick."

"A must-see for Kubrick acolytes," Empire Magazine wrote, before adding, "but the unconverted may find his last movie stylish but overblown." In a piece entitled Bedroom Odyssey, New York Times write Janet Maslin wrote a lengthy review. "Despite some abrupt editing in a work that the director never lived to fine-tune, the film moves effortlessly, and it goes straight under the skin. Its powerful and lingering resonance attests to a final compassion and profundity in Mr. Kubrick, the body-and-soul commitment of Mr. Cruise and Ms. Kidman, and the Rorschach-like ability of this material to envelop audiences in ways unexplained and unexpected."

For all the deserved praise we must heap on Kubrick for the individuality of this piece, a lot of credit surely needs to go to the undervalued power of Tom Cruise himself. He's in almost every scene, and gives the film its true soul. Through him we experience the bizarre and the enticing, the terrifying and the uncomfortable, and without his measured performance, the film may have veered off into the truly inaccessible, a freakshow of murder, sex and intrigue with no real thread. Roaming the quiet, haunted streets (though they are clearly New York streets, they are also universal avenues, and could in fact be anywhere in the world), Cruise puts in his most rounded effort to date, embodying all aspects of the modern male, with flaws and weakness included. It's a terribly complex, cubic portrayal of a jealous man, who is being consumed by his own newly discovered insecurities. He's a man who dares to go beneath the surface, the fake sheen that's there for all to see.

Everyone who sees Eyes Wide Shut will have their say on it. Though we can't hear Kubrick's take on the film, we can quote those who were closer to him. I believe Kubrick's brother in law and producer Jan Harlan summed the film up the best, when he said "it's not pornographic, it's about the mind, jealousy and sexual obsession of the mind." You may dissect the film's underlying themes, cryptic clues and hidden meanings, but at the end of the day, with Kubrick dead and unable to explain his motives, the only certainty we have is the simplistic summary Jan provides. Candia McWilliam, who collaborated on ideas for the script with Stanley early on in the project, commented the film was about the "mutual manipulation of jealousy. What we can do to one another in the most intimately painful way. If you are dealing with erotic entanglement there is a tendency to hurt." Maybe wouldn't have sold the film on the poster, but it sums it up pretty well.

For a filmmaker often criticised for his unhealthy depictions of sex and relationships in past movies (the sped up bonkathon in A Clockwork Orange apparently disturbed some people, and the marriage between Jack and Wendy in The Shining is painfully awkward from the word go), the relationship depicted in Eyes Wide Shut is obviously coming from a man who knew the dynamics between men and women very well. He was a man who knew the inner cogs and workings of a marriage, its darkest corners and least pleasant alleyways. Essentially, Nicole Kidman, in one of the best turns of her career, utters what is perhaps the most important line in the film: "If only you men knew." It's a brave line for a man to put in his movie. It cuts like a knife; and it has to be said, so does the film. Two decades on, in which time Kubrick has been long dead, Cruise and Kidman have split, Sydney Pollack has also passed away, and all manner of events and things have occurred in the world, Eyes Wide Shut seems to get better and better, getting more ambiguous as time floats by.

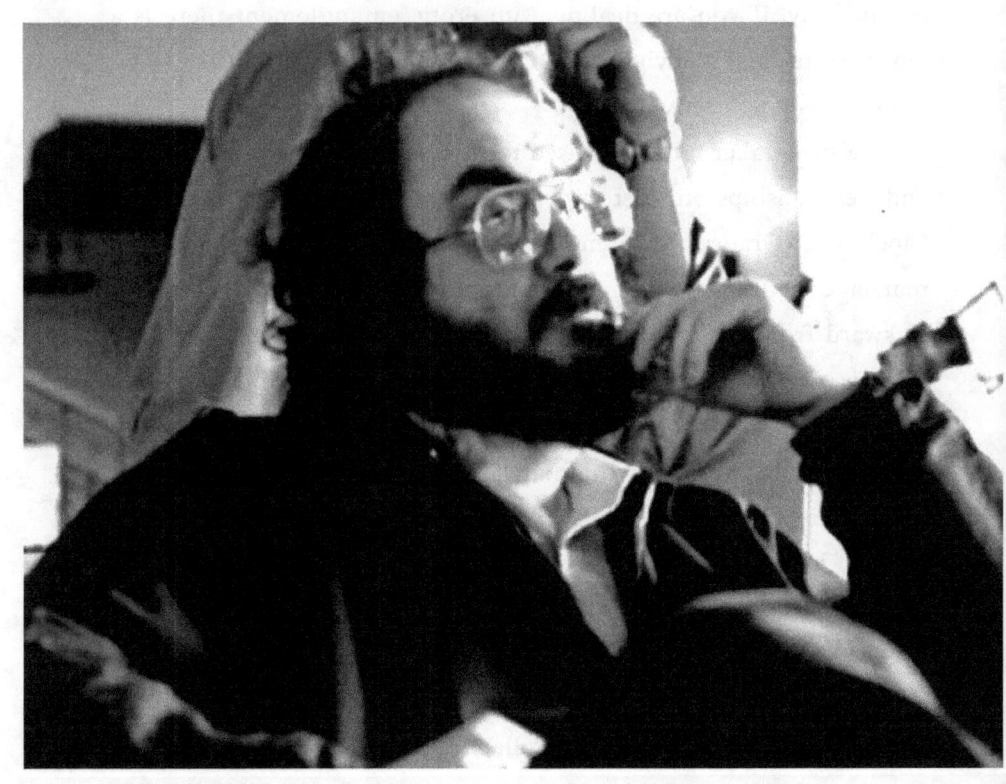

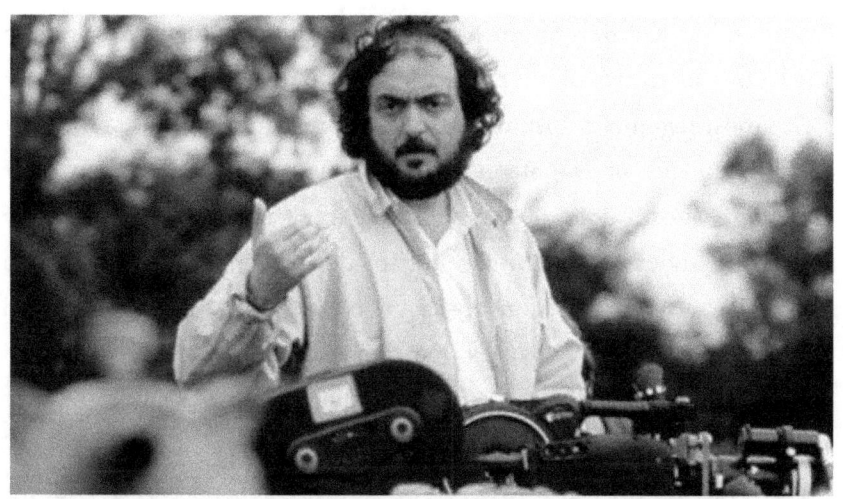

KUBRICK'S LOST FILMS

On the surface, or to those not in the know, Kubrick's 13 full length films in nearly fifty years could be seen as a slow, meagre workload. But the amount of work that went into one Kubrick movie adds up to ten by any other filmmaker. But even though 13 films is not that much, there were also a number of film projects Stanley began which sadly, for varying reasons, never went beyond the preparation stage.

The earliest of these unrealised films went all the way back to 1956, when he and his then business partner James B. Harris showed interest in Stefan Zweig's novel The Burning Secret. Kubrick had made three features at that point in time - Fear and Desire, Killer's Kiss and The Killing - and was yet to fully form his own unique style. The prospect of a drama about a young baron who seduces a Jewish woman by getting close to her twelve year old boy doesn't sound quite as exciting as Paths of Glory, a stonking war epic starring Kirk

Douglas, but Kubrick might have made an interesting film of this in the sixties, after provoking the world's moral code with Lolita.

The most legendary lost, unfinished Kubrick film was his attempt at filming the life of Napoleon, which he first approached right after the huge success of 2001. In a 1969 interview, Stanley was very optimistic about Napoleon coming to life in his hands. "We hope to begin the actual production work by the winter of 1969," he said, "and the exterior shooting - battles, location shots - should be completed within two or three months. After that, the studio work shouldn't take more than another three or four months."

However, in the same interview, Kubrick subconsciously admits that the film is not really a realistic possibility. The costs, the locations and the logistics, as Kubrick lists them off, just don't seem to come together. "Unfortunately, there are very, very few actual Napoleonic battlefields where we could still shoot; the land itself has either been taken over by industrial and urban development, pre-empted by historical trusts, or is so ringed by modern buildings that all kinds of anachronisms would present themselves. We intend to use a maximum of forty thousand infantry and ten thousand cavalry for the big battles, which means that we have to find a country which will hire out its own armed forces to us - you can just imagine the cost of fifty thousand extras over an extended period of time. Once we find a receptive environment, there are still great logistic problems -- for example, a battle site would have to be contiguous to a city or town or barracks area where the troops we'd use are already bivouacked. Let's say we're working with forty thousand infantry - if we could get forty men into a truck, it would still require a thousand trucks to move them around. So in addition to finding the proper terrain, it has to be within marching distance of military barracks."

In modern filmmaking times, the ambitious grand scale of Napoleon would be doable for a man of Kubrick's standing. CGI could be used to multiply the infantry, meaning there would be no need at all for 50,000 extras, and considerable money would be saved on reels of film, and he would therefore be more able to pump funds into costumes, battle scenes and authenticity. Back in the late 1960s though, Stanley's vision of Napoleon was, if not impossible, then very challenging indeed.

The amount of research he went into for the film is truly staggering when really taken in, even by Kubrick standards. It's well documented that he sent out researchers to get every single book on Napoleon, or even books featuring him, in every language from all over the world. In the end, Kubrick had gathered so much biographical detail on the man that he had a small cabinet with drawers in, which, when pulled out, revealed cue cards documenting what Napoleon did on every single day of his life. He even dispatched scouts to buy genuine Napoleon artefacts from France. At the time, the Paris riots were going on, and one can only giggle at the image of a mad eyed Kubrick researcher, running frantically through Paris with Napoleon's toilet in his arms, as bombs and guns are going off around him.

"He worked for two years on Napoleon," his brother in law and producer Jan Harlan explained, going into how the film project was abandoned. "That's how I started with him. It was MGM that pulled out. Dino de Laurentiis had greenlit a project called Waterloo with Rod Steiger as the lead. It was a Soviet-French-American co-production. MGM didn't want to take the risk of Kubrick following Waterloo with another expensive film – it was a business decision. Kubrick was very depressed for two weeks because he'd been gearing up to it and had become a scholar on the French Revolution. But then he moved on. The film would have fitted so well into his body of work. It was a film about a man who was colossally successful: he made France rich, was loved, had great charisma, but was a fool and vain and arrogant and had nobody to blame for his downfall other than himself. That's what was relevant for Kubrick because it still happens today."

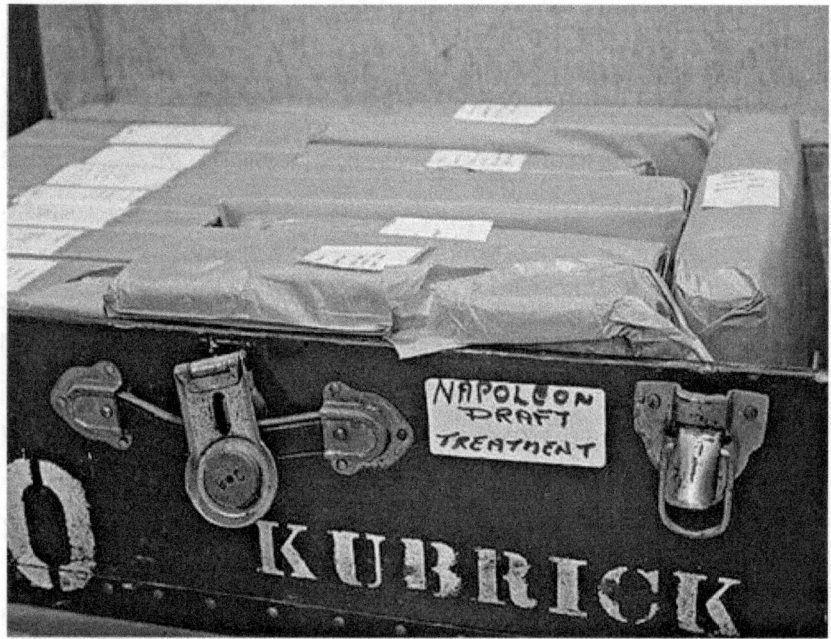

One can imagine how truly astounding Kubrick's Napoleon might have been. Add the vibrant, graceful beauty of Barry Lyndon and put in a lead character with the charisma and ego of Alex, the commanding presence of Sergeant Hartman from Full Metal Jacket and the dark menace of Jack Torrance and you have a pretty amazing character. Had Kubrick cast his original choice, Jack Nicholson, the possibilities would have been boundless. Alas, it was not to be.

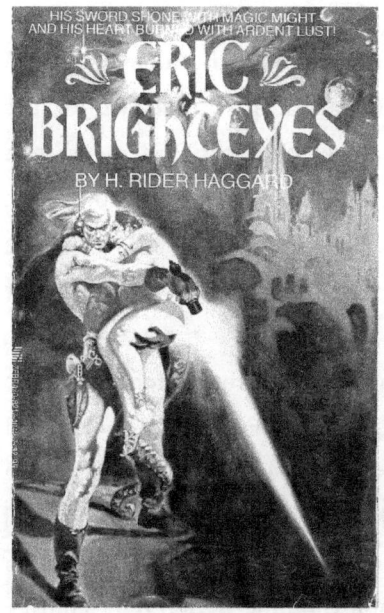

Anthony Frewin himself thinks that one uncompleted project in particular would have been brilliant for Stanley, citing it above Napoleon as the truly great lost Kubrick movie. "Eric Brighteyes is a dramatic three-pointed love triangle with plenty of action," Anthony told me. "It would have made a great film. Had Stanley Kubrick lived it could well have been his next film."

H Rider Haggard's epic Viking tale was written in 1890, and focuses on Eric as he tries to win over his true love, Gudruda. Her father, a high priest, is against the whole thing, so Eric enlists the help of a sorcerer to woo her heart. This fantasy adventure classic would have definitely made a great movie, and Kubrick might have been just the man to pull it off. Seeing as he never made a fantasy film, it is also very enticing to wonder how Stanley might have reinvented the whole genre. Again though, it never really got past consideration.

There are also screenplays which Kubrick actually completed himself but never got around to filming, like The German Lieutenant, all about a mission in the final days of the Second World

War. There's another oddity too, I Stole 16 Million Dollars, which was tipped to star Cary Grant. Again, nothing came of it.

Just after Full Metal Jacket saw release, he bought the rights to a story called Shadow on the Sun, a sci- fi tale that originated as a BBC radio serial, all about meteors crashing on the earth and spreading a deadly virus. The plot sounds more than a little like War of the Worlds, and in truth Kubrick would have made an amazing screen version of HG Wells' classic. (Ironically, that role went to Steven Spielberg in 2005.) He purchased screen rights for Shadow on the Sun from Gavin Blakeney, the writer of the series, but never developed it any further.

There was one very well known unfinished Kubrick movie. In the 12 year gap between the respective releases of Full Metal Jacket and Eyes Wide Shut, Kubrick spent years of his work time on a movie about the Holocaust. The idea went all the way back to the mid seventies, just after Barry Lyndon, when he asked Isaac Singer to pen a screenplay about the Holocaust. When the idea fizzled out, Kubrick put his obsession with the Holocaust on the back burner.

In the very early 1990s, he cleared room in his schedule for what would have been The Aryan Papers. It looks to have been a remarkable prospect, and he put his usual amount of time, money and attention into the development. He bought countless books on the period, stacks of them in fact, and read through them with such intensity that it began to trouble his wife and negatively affect his life. Becoming so emotionally involved in the horrors of the war, the concentration camps and the tragic plight of the Jewish people, Christiane would often find him slumped in the corner, crying, finding the whole thing too awful to bare. Understandably Christiane

144

later commented that she was relieved when he finally gave up on the project.

The actual plan was to adapt Louis Begley's Wartime Lies into The Aryan Papers, for which he planned to cast Uma Thurman as the Aunt fleeing Nazi Germany with her nephew. In the end, Kubrick lined up Johanna ter Steege as the Aunt and Jurassic Park star Joseph Mazzello as the child. As with Napoleon, it was the appearance of a "rival" film that killed off the Aryan Papers idea, in this case the monumental, multi Oscar wining Schindler's List, which Spielberg brought to the screen in 1993. Deflated, Kubrick abandoned the Aryan Papers for good.

As a side note, when working on Eyes Wide Shut with Frederic Raphael, the pair wondered if there had been any good Holocaust themed films. When Raphael mentioned Schindler's List, Kubrick, perhaps slightly bitter about the film's wide acclaim, apparently balked, "Think that's about the Holocaust? That was about success, wasn't it? The Holocaust is about 6 million people who get killed. Schindler's List is about 600 who don't. Anything else?" If Stanley ever really said that is anyone's guess, and the truth is buried with both men.

Perhaps Kubrick's most famous personally unrealised project was A.I. Artificial Intelligence, which he developed but passed on to Spielberg. Science fiction was an alluring area for an intellectual like Stanley, who had reinvented the genre with 2001, and was hoping one day to revisit it. (Not that he craved a sci-fi project in particular mind you.) Had he completed it, AI in the hands of Kubrick would have been a drastically different film to the one we ended up with.

He had first bought the screen rights to the original A.I. story, written by Brian Aldiss, in the early 1970s, and over the years, Stanley had hired various people to help him adapt it to the screen, but it never got past development. At one stage, Aldiss himself was hired to write the screen treatment, but Stanley eventually fired him from the project. Ian Watson also came on board, writing a version in the early 1990s. Kubrick lost interest in the idea while he was deeply immersed in Aryan Papers, and as CGI developed through the decade, began to regain confidence in bringing the complex science fiction tale to life. It was not until the mid 1990s though, that he and Spielberg decided to collaborate on the film, with Stanley as "producer" and Steven to direct.

"Stanley really fell in love with that story," producer Jan Harlan said to IGN, "but it was a short story and would never make a whole film, so he bought the rights and he developed it on his own and with other people into a big, comprehensive script. He did other things in between - he always took a lot of time - and in 1995, we were ready to go. During that time, he spoke with Steven Spielberg who was his friend anyway, and they spoke on the telephone a lot. But then he decided that this particular story would actually be better for Steven. A very unusual situation for a man like Kubrick, who was very, very high in his standing, professionally, but he was, at the same time, quite a humble fellow, and he figured that Steven would have the missing colours for this. He felt it was more his thing. So Steven came, and he showed him 650 drawings which he had, and the script and the story, everything, and said, 'Look. Why don't you direct it and I'll produce it?' Steven was almost in shock. He couldn't believe what he heard. And Stanley said, 'No, no, no, It's all right, It's all right. I think it will be a great thing. Can't you imagine? It'll be fabulous! A Stanley Kubrick Production of a Steven Spielberg Film. It sounds quite good to me.' And they laughed and horsed around, and Steven really liked the story, too."

Eventually, Kubrick put his focus on Eyes Wide Shut, which he worked on until his death, and Spielberg fully took over the project, eventually released in 2002 to a mixed reception. Kubrick's family admired the film, in particular his wife. Even Aldiss himself enjoyed the picture, despite the bitterness he felt at being dropped from his own project. "I thought what an inventive, intriguing, ingenious, involving film this was," he said, also contemplating on how Kubrick would have ended the movie. "That is one of the 'ifs' of film history - at least the ending indicates Spielberg adding some sugar to Kubrick's wine. The actual ending is overly sympathetic and moreover rather overtly engineered by a plot device that does not really bear credence. But it's a brilliant piece of film and of course it's a phenomenon because it contains the energies and talents of two brilliant filmmakers."

Of course, the difference between an unfinished project and a considered one is significant, and if we are talking "ideas" here, and material that was floating around under consideration, according to Mr Frewin there are "too many to mention." Frewin gave one away, saying that he once cast aside Bruce Robinson's script for The Killing Fields, saying it didn't hold his interest. And how about the idea of Kubrick directing The Beatles in an adaptation of Lord of the Rings; or a possible screen version of Peter Suskind's Perfume! With so many readers trawling through so many manuscripts, there are probably thousands of stories Stanley Kubrick could have brought to life.

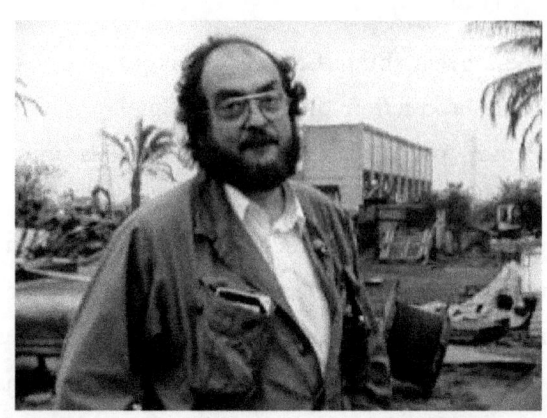

THE KUBRICK LEGACY

"I can't gainsay Stanley Kubrick's view on current cinema, but I would say he would have speedily embraced any new technology. No Luddite he." - Anthony Frewin to the author

Kubrick's name belongs to a very exclusive list, that of the truly great director, and he is without question in the top five of the most inspirational, innovative and influential filmmakers of all time. Since the start of moving pictures, no one had baffled, stunned, shocked and entertained with their films as he did. There have been more shocking directors, more commercial ones and much more succesful ones too, but none have balanced artistic integrity, financial success and technical wizardry quite like he. The list of completed works, though short, is in some ways the perfect filmography. After all, every genre was reassessed, and each film was an unprecedented achievement, every moment of which was carefully executed.

Stanley died in 1999, only a few days after finishing a cut of Eyes Wide Shut and showing it to Warners. Arguably his most mysterious, cloaked, secretive, curious and enigmatic movie, his sudden death and inevitable silence on the film's aims and themes has ensured it remains a strange, intriguing, indecipherable puzzle. Whether people be claiming it's about the Illuminati or rubbishing it as a dull drudge through snoozeville, everyone has their opinion on it; and everyone, for that matter, has an opinion on all of Kubrick's films, and the man himself too.

In his life time, particularly for the last twenty or so years, Kubrick was speculated and talked about in the press as if he were some hermit retreating from the world and everyone in it. In reality, he lived a functioning life, healthily, as a filmmaker and father, a husband and a friend. The egg wasn't cracked because there was nothing to crack. He didn't speak to the press, which of course leads the press into saying he didn't speak to anyone. "Having to defend the way you live" was, according to his daughter Katharina, a burden to Stanley and the family. He was a man who let his work do the talking for him, and you could learn a lot about Stanley Kubrick from watching one of his movies; which is quite a telling statement in itself, for these movies are, after all, cryptic and perplexing riddles, each one as inscrutable as the last. No wonder there was so much speculation about his "secret" life.

It's inevitable that the legend of Kubrick is only bound to deepen over time, coupling together his so called "reclusive" state and the extraordinary art he made for every subsequent generation to enjoy. One without the other is enough to ensure a filmmaker goes down in history, but Stanley has the honour of being both a conundrum and a genius to his legion of fans. The influence he has had on other filmmakers cannot be overstated either, for much of modern film would not exist in the way it does had it not been for him.

There is now a whole sub genre in film, "Kubrickian," and there are whole lists of movies which are directly influenced by his style. The name Kubrick is synonymous with high quality, perfectionism and to cite him as an influence is not only a statement on Kubrick himself, but on the filmmaker who is citing him. To attach your name to his is a bold move, but hundreds of directors have lifted ideas from his work.

Christopher Nolan is one modern director who repeatedly offers up his views on Kubrick's brilliance. Rather than comparing himself to Kubrick, as only a fool would, Nolan points out how he learns from watching Stanley's films and sees his own weaknesses when putting them aside his own. "From a storytelling point of view, from a directing point of view, there is one thing I associate with what Kubrick does, which is *calm*," Nolan said "There is such an inherent calm and inherent trust of the one powerful image, that he makes me embarrassed with my own work, in terms of how many different shots, how many different sound effects, how many different things we'll throw at an audience to make an impression. But with Kubrick, there is such a great trust of the one correct image to calmly explain something to the audience. There can be some slowness to the editing. There's nothing frenetic about it. It's very simple. There's a trust in simple storytelling and simple image making that actually takes massive confidence to try and emulate. I think any time you look at science fiction in movies, there are key touchstones, Metropolis. Blade Runner, 2001. Whenever you're talking about

150

getting off the planet, 2001 is somewhat unavoidable. But there is only one 2001. So you don't want to get too near to that."

To list all the directors who have learned from his films would seem endless. The obvious ones are Quentin Tarantino, Sam Mendes, David Fincher, Guillermo Del Toro and David Lynch, who from him learned how to combine the sublime and the surreal, the masterful shot with the art of editing, imagery and music; not to mention the jagged narratives. Kubrick broke so many rules that he made new rules all of his own, ones we are still following nearly twenty years after his death.

The use of music is one specific area where Kubrick really changed the game. Alongside the likes of Dennis Hopper with Easy Rider and Martin Scorsese with Mean Streets, Kubrick was responsible for the film soundtrack revolution that started in the 1960s and 70s. When he really got cooking, he started to use pre-existing music to enhance the power of his sequences. This book has highlighted time and again the importance of Kubrick's sheer power with imagery, but one cannot understate the impact the music has on those visuals. Think of the nuclear bomb exploding in Dr Strangelove without Vera Lynn's We'll Meet Again; imagine 2001 without the music of Strauss; A Clockwork Orange without Beethoven's powerhouse compositions and Wendy/Walter Carlos's cosmic, moog reshaping of them; The Shining without the eerie, other worldly music that floats through the film like a ghost in itself; Full Metal Jacket without the sixties rock songs which so encapsulate the 'Nam era; and what would Eyes Wide Shut be without its minimalist score or Chris Isaak's baby Did A Bad Bad Thing?

Kubrick uses music as a main ingredient in the mix. Sound, vision and dialogue are equally important, but music is the key to what gives a shot like the blood bursting from the elevator in The Shining its true power. The comical sex scene in A Clockwork Orange would not have been quite so hilarious and ahead of its time if not for the high speed Beethoven on the soundtrack. For all their hype, Tarantino's supposedly revolutionary movie soundtracks have got nothing on Kubrick's innovative use of music in all its various styles and forms, not simply as homage, but as a cinematic enhancement.

He's been dead for nearly two decades now, but his films continue to grow, evolve and reshape themselves. The fact he's not tied to one particular genre makes him the master of them all. As the late Sydney Pollack defined it, he had to have the best or most extreme example of whatever he was aiming for; the scariest horror film; the most violent fight scene; the most erotic bedroom scene; the funniest comedy; the grittiest war picture. Each and every idea, second and frame had to be executed to its fullest potential, and always delivered maximum power to the viewer.

In an age of heartless superhero films, CGI mega-feasts, gory horror trash, idiotic gross out comedies and half baked studio dross, films of the quality of which Kubrick crafted are relics of the past. We don't get masterpieces like those anymore because the studios won't allow them, and no filmmaker is willing to sacrifice fame and money for his own personal integrity as Kubrick did. They're following the popular trends rather than defining them. Without wanting to sound out dated, Stanley Kubrick will forever be a name that defines what a quality film is, and we'll never see the likes of him ever again.

References and Acknowledgements

Thanks to Dan Richter, Doug Milsome and Stanley's long time assistant Anthony Frewin for answering my questions.

The sources cited below were invaluable in completing this book.

Stanley Kubrick: A Life in Pictures

Stanley Kubrick's Boxes

The Art of Stanley Kubrick

Stanley Kubrick Remembered

The Making of 2001

The Making of A Clockwork Orange

Books;

Director: A Visual Analysis, Alexander Walker

The Cinema of Stanley Kubrick, Norman Kagen

Studies in the Horror Film: Stanley Kubrick's The Shining

The Stanley Kubrick Archives

Stanley Kubrick: A Biography, John Baxter

Eyes Wide Open, by Frederic Raphael

Stanley Kubrick Companion

Stanley Kubrick: The Complete Films

The Complete Kubrick, by David Hughes

ABOUT CHRIS WADE

Chris Wade is a UK based writer, filmmaker and musician. As well as running the acclaimed music project Dodson and Fogg, he has written books on The Kinks, Captain Beefheart, Robert De Niro and many more. He has also released audiobooks of his comedic fiction, narrated by such actors as Rik Mayall. His first film is The Apple Picker, featuring Nigel Planer and Toyah Willcox.

More info at his website: wisdomtwinsbooks.weebly.com

Email: wisdomtwinsbooks@hotmail.com

www.ingramcontent.com/pod-product-compliance
Lightning Source LLC
Chambersburg PA
CBHW071434180526
45170CB00001B/345